BEASTLY
NUISANCES

BEASTLY NUISANCES

COPING WITH GARDEN PESTS

THE ESSENTIAL GUIDE

Val Porter

Illustrations by Robin Morton-Smith

ROBSON BOOKS

First published in Great Britain in 2003 by Robson Books, The Chrysalis Building, Bramley Road, London W10 6SP

An imprint of Chrysalis Books Group plc

The author has made every reasonable effort to contact all copyright holders. Any errors that may have occurred are inadvertent and anyone who for any reason has not been contacted is invited to write to the publishers so that a full acknowledgement may be made in subsequent editions of this work.

British Library Cataloguing in Publication Data
A catalogue record for this title is available from the British Library.

ISBN 1 86105 604 4

Typeset by SX Composing DTP, Rayleigh, Essex
Printed by Creative Print & Design (Wales),
Ebbw Vale

Contents

Introduction

My country garden is surrounded by pasture and woodland and is deliberately maintained as a haven for most of the wildlife that chooses to live within its boundaries. I *like* wildlife – even the 'nuisances' such as wasps and spiders and yellow-neck mice – and I appreciate that, from their point of view, I am invading their territory, not the other way round. Usually I tolerate, or indeed actively encourage, the presence of a wide range of birds, mammals, reptiles, amphibians and insects: partly because their lives and activities are interesting to watch; partly because they generally settle into a good natural balance and can help my gardening as much as hinder it; and partly because I feel they have just as much right to be here as I do – especially when their living space is shrinking year by year in a small country where humans are so omnipresent, dominant and intolerant.

There is a deep-seated human urge to control nature and to establish a territory over which that control can be exerted. It worries us when animals don't behave themselves – when domestic pets and livestock don't do as we wish, or when wild creatures take liberties and ignore our hollow threats. It worries us even more when they 'pester' us, especially if they enter our homes. We begin to think in an arrogant way that they are deliberately coming into conflict with us, provoking us, almost teasing us by ignoring our wishes. From the animal's point of view, our gardens and homes make ideal environments; the fact that humans live there as well is almost incidental. But we do live there, and we do sometimes find the presence of other species intolerable, especially where their habits are destructive.

I'm all for diversity and living together, though preferably not inside my own cottage! There are limits even in the garden. I decided enough was enough when a wild doe rabbit attempted for the third dawn running to dig her birthing burrow exactly under a newly planted shrub – the same spot she had tried three weeks earlier, and another three weeks before that. Death wasn't the aim – just a mutual respect. But this doe was determined that the only place to dig her nursery stop was in my border within a yard of the cottage walls and right under a window, despite the fact that she had a wide choice of secluded, peaceful woodland, warm grassland and dry hedgebanks where she could safely dig and give birth and nurture her young undisturbed. The previous year another doe had concentrated with equal persistence on a particular spot in the vegetable patch, under a self-sown borage plant.

I tried everything to dissuade these rabbits: obnoxious smells, high-frequency sound emitters, gorse carpets, raids at five o'clock in the morning to catch them in the act, general disturbance, welcoming the neighbour's cat and a host of tricks picked up over the years. After some fifteen years of battling half-heartedly with the rabbits by netting the vegetable patch and every flower bed, I finally rabbit-proofed the whole garden, with rabbit netting along every boundary. It was really no more expensive than dealing with the problem on a piecemeal basis year after year and getting unhealthily irritated by the persistence of the rabbits. But it was an acknowledgement of defeat; with none of the other creatures in my garden, or those that venture into the cottage, have I needed to go to such an extreme. The rest of us do manage to live in harmony, and they give me at least an illusion that I am sometimes in control.

In the past, the reaction to such frustration has been to kill; if you read old gardening books and country journals, you will find endless ways of eradicating 'pests'. Perhaps we have become a little more enlightened, or less dependent on garden produce as an important part of our diet. Perhaps we have realised that wholesale slaughter is not the answer, that we need to strike a balance, bargain with nature, accommodate other species and 'control' them by guile rather than by force.

Years ago, I read a short story (and I apologise to the author for not remembering his or her name) about an old woman, recently widowed, who had a morbid terror of spiders. Her husband had always dealt with them on her behalf but now she lived alone and had no one to remove them for her. The autumn rains came and the first of the big ones entered her house. So she faced up to the reality and went to the local library on the basis that fear springs from ignorance. She read everything she could about spiders and suddenly found them interesting. Indeed, she ended up as a national authority on spiders and a converted arachnophile; not only had she conquered her fear, but also found she had a new lease of life.

My hope is that this book will give you enough knowledge of the ordinary life of your particular 'pests' to feel less threatened by them, and will encourage you to pause before you whip out the chemicals or swat those irritating insects. There are other ways! Try a bit of human ingenuity, and if you must have a battle, make it a battle of wits, not a battle to the death.

Rabbit Rabbit

Those who live near chalk downland will appreciate the value of rabbits in the landscape. If it were not for their close grazing of downland turf, the downs would be invaded by scrub and trees and the terrain would be quite different. There would be none of the many beautiful and often rare little flowering plants that add to the magic of downland: the rabbits leave bare areas of soil in which those plants can germinate and grow and it is the rabbits that keep the grass short enough not to overwhelm the flowers. The same is true in many areas of heathland where conservation is in progress: without rabbits, the heather might soon be overgrown by shrubs and birch. The rabbits nibble down seedling shrubs and trees so that they never have a chance to grow and dominate the heath.

Of course, rabbits are not saints. Rabbits, as everybody knows, breed like rabbits. In the pre-myxamatosis days, the rabbits of Britain were rampant and there were about a hundred million of them – virtually two rabbits for every human being in the country. The countryside was heaving with them and they had become pests rather than assets. In the early 1950s, some 40 million rabbits were being killed annually in a concerted drive to reduce the huge amount of damage they were doing to crops and newly planted trees.

When the myxy virus arrived in 1953, it wiped out 99 per cent of the existing population. But you can't keep a good rabbit down and over the last fifty years their numbers have been relentlessly increasing, despite being one of Nature's most sought-after victims for a wide range of predators, whether on four legs, four wheels, two legs or two wings, or even no legs at all in the case of reptiles.

With so many gunning for the gentle, soft-eyed rabbit, does it not make you think twice about joining the throng when rabbits bless you with their presence in your garden? After all, in most gardens it is hardly a matter of economic disaster – damage, yes, and aggravation too, but surely not a threat to the very lives of you and your family.

RABBIT HABITS

Rabbits are nearly, but not quite, rodents. They have incisor teeth that must always be gnawing if these are not to grow unhealthily long but, unlike those of true rodents, their second upper incisors are behind the first ones rather than beside them.

Rabbits have a peculiar digestive system that lets them cope with the fibrous material of grasses. Whereas cows deal with the coarseness of cellulose in grasses by having four stomachs and regurgitating their food for further chewing and digesting, a rabbit has just one stomach but it recycles its own droppings. The first pellets it excretes are moist and the rabbit immediately eats them for further digestion to extract more goodness from its food. It is the second, recycled pellets that are scattered about the place as droppings – or tiddlings, or whatever other local dialect name you care to give them.

With so many predators around, rabbits are always in a state of high alert. Their field of vision is a full 360°, so they will always see you coming and be off like a shot. They also have acute senses of smell and hearing, and a highly developed social alarm system. They are mainly creatures of the night and twilight, and are particularly twitchy on moonlit nights. They don't particularly like getting their belly-fur wet but a shower on their backs is easily shaken off.

Grub

A fully grown wild rabbit weighs between 1 and 2kg (2 and 4lb) and eats about a third of that body weight in green food every day. That is a lot of lettuce! What rabbits really like are nutritious, juicy young shoots of grass or cereal crops, but they are far from fussy – almost anything green will do, and many other titbits too. In the garden they head straight for wallflowers, peas, beans, brassicas, salad crops, carrots, windfall apples (however inedibly green) and even potatoes, with a quick nibble of the strawberries and raspberries for afters. In winter, when conditions are hard, they will gnaw off the bark of apple trees and browse on the shoots of shrubs.

They have an infuriating habit of neatly clipping off your favourite flowers low down on the stem and leaving them to wilt on the ground, not even bothering to eat them, in what seems like almost wilful destruction. Sometimes it is just a matter of trying something in case it tastes good, and quite often they will immediately spot anything that has just been planted and give it a go, even though they might ignore the same species of plant if it has been growing there for some time. Curiosity, perhaps, or a need to make their mark on the garden?

Feeling at home

Rabbits were originally animals of semi-arid areas and in Europe they were mainly found in southern France and the Iberian peninsula. They were deliberately introduced into Britain in Norman times and are, strictly speaking, feral rather than wild: they descended from animals that had been kept and bred in captivity. However, that was so long ago – back in the Roman period in Europe – that they have had plenty of time to adapt to wildness.

The ideal habitat for rabbits in Britain is in drier areas, particularly on easily worked sandy soils where they can dig to their hearts' content. A well-drained burrow is important, and a bank, embankment or sheltered hillside is always a promising site. Best of all is short grassland close to good cover, so that they can hide in hedgerows, scrub, brambles, the edge of woodland, under or between rocks, or anywhere else where they can make a safe warren of burrows to escape from countless predators. They only feel comfortable feeding within about 50m (160ft) of the burrows, though food scarcities will force them farther afield.

Rabbits do not like long grass and rank vegetation; the young, in particular, cannot survive if they get soaking wet in long grass. Nor do rabbits like digging into heavy clays or waterlogged peat. They are not happy in the middle of dense, mature conifer plantations either, nor in the middle of heavy deciduous woodland.

Home for rabbits has always been the warren – a social city of burrows, where they can interact and doze and rear their young out of sight. Long-established warrens, which may have existed for centuries, can become quite complex and extensive and form the core of a complicated colony system in which every rabbit knows its place. In pre-myxy days, rabbits tended to stay in their burrows during the day (emerging mainly to feed under cover of darkness or in the twilight hours) but experience taught them that burrows were ideal for harbouring the fleas that were largely responsible for spreading the dreaded myxy virus, so some of them took to lying up on the surface, hidden by undergrowth, crops and grass, rather like their cousin, the hare.

Spring is in the air . . .

The mating season for Britain's rabbits now seems to be virtually all year round. Does (females) are perfectly capable of having half a dozen batches of babies during the year, with anything up to ten babies in each batch. They have a system of continuous oestrus, in which ovulation is induced by copulation. A doe can become pregnant again just a day or two after giving birth. The gestation period is about four weeks. Most does in a colony will be pregnant between late January and May, but many will continue to produce babies even in the early months of winter, though the chances of their survival are greatly reduced.

Rabbits give birth underground. While many does will make nests for their young in a side chamber of the main warren, others search elsewhere for somewhere safe and undisturbed (like a corner of your garden, where you've just kindly cleared the ground and turned the soil for them) and dig themselves a 'stop' – a sloping tunnel perhaps a metre (yard) or two long, with a cosy nest at the far end. About a week before giving birth, the doe begins to line her nest with grass or moss, and in the last two days before the birth she plucks fur from her own belly to make the final cushioning.

At birth, the nestlings are blind and only sparsely furred. The doe leaves them in the nest and will visit them only once in every 24 hours, staying for less than five minutes to give them a chance to suckle frantically before she disappears again, carefully plugging the entrance to foil predators. After about three weeks she leaves the entrance open, to encourage the little ones to come out; by then they are already partially weaned, and within a few days she deserts them, leaving them entirely to their own devices while she gets on with the business of making a new nest for the next lot.

The enemies

The youngsters themselves are capable of breeding by the age of four months, if they survive that long. Most live for less than a year, though exceptionally a lucky rabbit might live more than five years. They are preyed upon by stoats, ferrets, foxes, wild cats, badgers, domestic cats, snakes, buzzards – in fact, almost anything that likes an easy meal. Young rabbits face a whole host of other problems too: they might starve in a drought or a harsh winter; they might drown in a badly sited burrow; they might get chewed up by farm machinery as they hide in the hay or corn; they might die of exposure after a soaking in heavy rain; they might be abandoned by a busy mum before they have been weaned; or they might have their habitat destroyed. It is amazing that as many as 10 per cent of the young survive into their first autumn. Of course rabbits of all ages are killed by human beings, either deliberately, or accidentally on the roads. Then, as well as myxy and the more recent rabbit viral haemorrhagic disease (RVHD) that reached Britain in the mid-1990s, rabbits are host to countless parasites inside and out.

And you still want to kill them? Yes, they can be a nuisance: they bark your trees; they prune your flowers; they nibble your plants; they dig nest-holes in your vegetable patch; they mock you when you shout at them – but *kill* them? There are other ways of dealing with their vexations.

FINGERING THE CULPRIT

You need to be sure that the damage in your garden is really being caused by rabbits. If you have not actually seen a rabbit in the act, here are the signs.

- The **track** is distinctive: the back feet are much longer than the front ones.
- The **trail** is also distinctive. Rabbits move by hopping, not walking, and the hops might be about 20 to 30cm (8 to 12in) apart, though this depends on whether the animal is moving at leisure or bounding away at speed. At a leisurely hop, you will see two small roundish marks for the forefeet just ahead of two elongated teardrops or sausages for the hind feet; one forefoot might be slightly ahead of the other. At a run, it looks as if the hind feet are ahead of the forefeet, and the latter might be just a set of four claw prints lightly touching the ground as the animal races away.

Trail of a running rabbit

- **Nibbling** is very clean-cut, as if someone had taken a sharp pair of secateurs to a stem or shoot (deer leave a more ragged cut).
- **Gnawing** on trees and fallen branches is betrayed by toothmarks from the paired front incisor teeth. The rabbits actually eat the bark, whereas squirrels simply strip it and leave it lying around.
- **Droppings** are round to slightly oval pellets, each completely separate from the others and usually less than 1cm (½in) in diameter (size and texture depend on what the animal has been eating and its own body size). Fresh droppings are dark in colour; older pellets eventually become light khaki or straw-coloured. The droppings often accumulate in piles at special latrine areas; you might find them on a flat stone, for example, or simply plonked on the lawn, or just a couple deposited in a scrape in the ground.
- **Urine** patches are sometimes visible as wet marks on soil or snow.
- Snags of **fur** might be found on barbed-wire fences or caught by hedge twigs. The hairs are soft and flecked.
- The **smell** of a rabbit can only be described as rabbity and will be instantly recognised by anybody who has ever kept a pet rabbit. Sometimes a smell is the only evidence you will find to indicate that there is or was a rabbit nearby.
- The **noise** of a rabbit is minimal. Rabbits don't chatter and squeak like many other mammals, though occasionally they might grunt and they can emit the most spine-

chilling high scream if caught by a predator. The most likely sound of a rabbit is the characteristic thumping of the back legs on the ground as a warning to all its friends that there is danger close by.

LIKES AND DISLIKES

A rabbit's likes and dislikes are the key to managing rabbit invasions in your garden. The 'likes' are what attracted the animals to the garden in the first place. As with most 'pests', these include food, shelter (from weather and predators), somewhere to mate, somewhere to hide and rear their babies, and, in general, peace and quiet to go about their business unmolested. If you tire of the pleasure of rabbit-watching, your aim should be either not to supply the 'likes' or to prevent rabbits from making use of them.

- Rabbits do not like grazing in dirty areas and you could always try to deter them by applying manure on any bare soil or perhaps sprinkling sheep droppings on the lawn (with the added advantage of this being a useful fertiliser). Liquid cow manure sprayed on soil or grass is effective but much messier than sheep tiddlings. Alternatively, cover vulnerable areas with something prickly such as chopped-up gorse or dry holly leaves (if you can stop them from blowing away in the wind).
- Apparently, rabbit urine from a buck (male) will deter other males from entering the area, but unfortunately it just might attract the does – which could mean baby rabbits in your garden.
- Human urine is another deterrent and old countrymen used to 'take a leak' along their garden boundaries last

thing at night to warn off rabbits and other undesirable night visitors; sometimes the dog joined in this nightly 'marking' of the territory.

- Your local zoo might be able to sell you some lion excrement, which seems to scare off rabbits – even though they wouldn't recognise a lion if they met one.
- There are various chemical deterrents on the market and some of them do work, but the smells can be equally disgusting to humans. Can you put up with the stink yourself?
- An old country trick is to set quart-sized wide-mouthed jars around smallish plots (say 6 × 6m, or 20 × 20ft); apparently they 'rumble' when the wind blows across them, scaring the rabbits.
- The best deterrents are probably predators, which you can encourage as long as you don't find that they, too, become a nuisance in the garden. Predation by the rabbit's natural enemies is the best way of maintaining a sensible balance. Stoats, weasels, foxes, badgers and other wild mammals, and your local buzzards if you are lucky enough to have them, should be made welcome.
- You could invest in your own domestic predators: a terrier, for example, or a hunting cat.
- Try planting a border of the herb, rue, or of elder – two plants that rabbits really do not like at all. You could poke elder cuttings or branches into the ground to protect individual plants or groups. Bamboo is another useful living fence against rabbits. A list of other plants that rabbits do not usually eat, though you can never really generalise about rabbits, is given in the box.
- Keep the grass and other vegetation around the edge of the garden as long as possible (if you can prevent the rabbits from grazing it down) and keep that grass wet.

- Protect individual saplings with tree-guards (talk to your local forester).
- Investigate the possibility of birth control. People have been working for years on contraceptives for doe rabbits and on ways of sterilising the bucks (including a hormone that switches off their sex drive) but the practicalities of getting your rabbits to take 'the pill' are tricky.

Plants that rabbits might not eat

Most rabbits will not eat or even try to eat the following plants, but some rabbits seem to have a go at just about anything, even if they don't eat it. Very broadly, most do not go for berry-producing plants, thorny plants, poisonous plants or bulb foliage/flowers.

- **Wild plants:** elder and bramble; bracken and fern; nettle, thistle, ragwort, foxglove, scarlet pimpernel, goutweed (ground elder).
- **Garden shrubs:** laurel, box, large-leaved evergreen rhododendron (but rabbits will happily prune small-leaved azaleas); viburnum, philadelphus, lilac, clematis.
- **Bulbs:** daffodils, tulips and other bulbs (but some will graze off the leaves of grape hyacinths).
- **Garden herbaceous plants:** peony, hypericum, periwinkle; pelargoniums (though rabbits might take off and discard a few leaves on newly planted ones, and they will certainly graze the true geraniums and cranesbills); lily-of-the-valley (but some will eat them); cyclamen, yellow flag, aconitum, ajuga, alchemilla, pulmonaria, red-hot poker, sweet william (if you are lucky), hemerocallis (day lily, said to be hallucogenic for rabbits), cannabis/hemp, comfrey.

KEEPING THEM OUT

If none of the deterrents works, the next step is protection. It is important to bear in mind that rabbits are expert diggers-under, good jumpers and also clever climbers. What usually happens is that you set up some sort of fencing and somehow a rabbit finds its way in but resolutely refuses to find its way out again.

- Erect temporary electric fencing (mesh, rabbit-size) around vulnerable areas. The rabbit's feet are well insulated by fur and rabbits quite happily slip under plain electric-wire fencing used for confining cattle, for example.
- Go the whole hog and fence the entire garden permanently. This will be expensive in the short run but in the long term will save you much frustration, emotional capital and money wasted on devastated plants. You need strong wire mesh and solid field fencing stakes. The netting should be 18g 31mm (⅔oz 1in) mesh and the fence needs to be at least 1m (3ft) high, with at least a further 15cm (6in) of the mesh buried and extending horizontally outwards to prevent the rabbit from digging down and under the fence. (They tend to start digging at the base of a fence and don't seem to be able to work out that a horizontal barrier doesn't extend for ever, so they don't back off and start digging further away but simply give up when they meet the opposition.) The top of the fence, ideally, should have a T-bar to thwart climbers and swarmers, in which case you might be able to get away with a slightly lower fence. There should anyway be horizontal straining wires at the top, middle and base of the fence.

Baby rabbits are able to get through unbelievably tiny gaps and are remarkably good climbers as well – I have seen them swarming their way up and over wire netting as if they were born storm-troopers. They are also good at becoming invisible and refusing to bolt, so that you have no idea they are there.

THE LAST RESORT

In theory, the occupier of the land is obliged to control any rabbits that are on it, or at least to prevent them from damaging a neighbour's crops, but few landowners these days seem to bother with rabbit control. If it really does come down to control as a last resort, those with appropriate skill and licences can use shooting, ferreting, trapping, gassing or poisoning. You should, however, talk to a professional warrener if the problem is bad enough to warrant such drastic action. It will be a permanent war.

It is possible, with skill and persistence, to 'live-trap' rabbits but most of them are far too wily to fall for the lure of chopped-up carrots or other tasty bait. If you do decide on live-trapping, you must visit the trap often to make sure that no rabbit is left there in a state of what will be extreme distress for any longer than necessary. And then, of course, you have to decide what to do with your caught rabbit. Perhaps you could give up the unequal struggle and decide that, if rabbits like your garden so much, you might as well become a warrener of the old kind and invite them in, creating a really good home for them and making an asset out of a 'pest'.

HARES

Make sure your rabbit isn't a hare. Hares are larger than rabbits and have black tips to their ears. They have proportionately longer hind legs, tend to lope and are very fast runners. Unlike rabbits, hares tend to be solitary, or might be in pairs in the breeding season or in small groups. They are famous for their 'mad March' behaviour, with a lot of energetic chasing, leaping around and 'boxing' each other. They don't bother with warrens and usually lie up in a 'form' (a shallow depression in long grass, etc.); the young (leverets) are born above ground, their eyes are wide open and they have a full fur coat at birth.

I once reared a leveret: its mother had made her open nest in my front garden in Maryland, USA, when I lived adjacent to a busy dual carriageway. One of the little ones was always being pushed out of the nest, so eventually I adopted it and handfed it for a month, following instructions from a local zoo. A great success – until it managed to fall to its death down the fireplace's ash shaft into the basement.

Rabbit's front and hind footprints

Deer Raiders

Isn't it a shame deer eat roses and trees? If it wasn't for that, everybody would simply admire their beauty and love them.

In Britain, there are two native species of deer and several that were originally introduced from other countries and have since escaped from enclosed parks and zoological gardens to take up residence in freedom. The true natives are the red deer and the roe; the escapees are fallow, sika, muntjac and water deer.

The **red deer** is the big one – the 'Monarch of the Glen' beast of the Scottish Highlands, with a few herds in scattered areas of England. A Scottish stag, resplendent in his branching antlers, might stand at more than 120cm (4ft) tall at the shoulder. The red deer is usually an animal of the uplands and moorlands; it is more of a grazer than a browser (though, like other deer, it is very happy to rip bark from trees in winter) and is essentially a herd animal, usually with the sexes segregated.

The next largest is the **fallow**, an elegant parkland herd species that typically has a spotted coat and flattened antlers. The main herds are in southern and eastern England but they can be found all over England and in many parts of Scotland, Ireland and Wales too.

The **sika** is heavily spotted but its horns are not flattened. I once came across one in the depths of the New Forest and I thought at first it was somebody's idea of a joke. All I saw, in the gloaming, was its head; it was utterly motionless, as if it had been stuffed and mounted. We were within a few paces of each other and I had caught it in mid-wallow (it likes a damp environment). The sika, which is more of a grazer than a browser, originated in Japan but there are a few feral herds in Britain. Numbers have increased rapidly in recent years and there are concerns because it is able to hybridise with the native red deer.

The **roe** (male average height about 65cm or 2ft 2in) is the other British native; it almost became extinct in the early eighteenth century and European animals were introduced to boost its numbers. The roe is now widespread and common throughout Scotland and northern England, and also found in large numbers in southern and parts of eastern England. It tends to live in small family groups, often the doe with her (usually) twin youngsters. The males have prong-type horns rather than the elaborate branches of red and fallow deer; at the most an adult male will have just a couple of tines on the prongs. There are all sorts of uses for the shed prongs you sometimes find in the woods: they make handy dibbers for planting bulbs and transplanting leeks, or handles for thumbsticks. The roe is a dainty, pretty animal and a charmer but it can drive gardeners and foresters to distraction.

The strange little **Chinese water deer** has no antlers: it has tusks, and big, rounded ears. Male water deer are up to about 60cm (2ft) tall. The species escaped originally from Woburn Abbey Deer Park in Bedfordshire; ferals can be found mainly in Bedfordshire, with a few elsewhere that have escaped from various zoos over the years. In their native land they live in swampy habitats; in Britain they are quite happy with grassland.

Slightly smaller, the equally strange **muntjac** or barking deer is also Chinese in origin. It has an oddly rounded back and when I first met one in my local woods, I thought it was a dog, pottering along the track with nose to the ground as if following a scent. It didn't notice me until it had almost bumped into me – then it shot away up the slope through the trees at a tremendous pace, barking more like a dog than a roe. It has tusks; the male also has rather plain antlers growing upwards in a peculiar fashion from extended, fur-covered, knobby frontal bones. Its facial expression always seems to be rather worried and it is quite secretive, prefer-ring the cover of woodland, but it does sometimes come out into the open, even in broad daylight. I noticed one after-noon that the sheep in the meadow edging my garden were looking not concerned but interested and eventually I spotted a muntjac slipping nonchalantly through the long grass and then melting into the bracken-carpeted copse at

Muntjac deer

the top of the garden. You are unlikely to see a muntjac unless you live in the Midlands, East Anglia or southern England; and, again, it is likely to be a Woburn escapee by origin.

ON THE TRAIL

You need evidence that deer have been at work in your garden rather than just rabbits and squirrels, who might wreak what is at first sight similar damage. First of all, rabbits leave a clean oblique line when they prune buds and shoots, whereas deer leave rough, chewed-looking edges. Rabbits generally nibble rather than strip bark, in small pieces while the trees are dormant, and leave parallel oblique toothmarks. Deer strip or fray (rub against the bark, leaving it hanging off the tree in strips) rather than nibble it, in both winter and summer. Their winter bark-stripping is well defined with more or less vertical parallel toothmarks. Summer stripping is in vertical bands; fraying might be down just one side, leaving score marks on the wood beneath, or might be all round, leaving twisted and broken branches as well. The height of the damage varies according to the species of deer.

Trail of a running roe deer –
a strolling deer's prints usually overlap

Deer are cloven-hoofed and the track is described as a 'slot', each hoofmark being a pair of slightly curved, raindrop-shaped indentations. Sheep and goats leave similar prints and are just as likely to browse in your garden given the chance.

Droppings of some species might initially be confused with those of rabbits. Muntjac pellets tend to be about 1cm (½in) long, black and slightly elongated; those of red deer are twice the size and anything from light brown to black, usually bottle-shaped (cylindrical, flat at one end and pointed at the other); those of fallow are also black and bottle-shaped, about 1.5cm (¾in) long; those of sika are like small black currants; those of roe are oval, 1.5 to 2cm (less than an inch) long and usually black; and those of water deer are black but cigar-shaped.

You don't usually need to resort to working out whether deer are the culprits by examining the droppings. You'll probably see the deer in the flesh, at twilight or even in broad daylight, caught in the act at the scene of the crime. The most likely garden invaders are roe, fallow and, increasingly, muntjac. They don't seem to be particularly bothered by the presence of humans and some of them happily continue to munch your plants while you stand just yards away, even in daylight or when floodlights suddenly come on.

Deer nibbles

In the wild, red deer mainly graze on grass, sedges and reeds, or, in winter, browse on heather, holly and conifers (including bark). They also nibble at new young leaves and shoots on deciduous shrubs and trees, and might eat herbs, ferns, lichen and fungi. Fallow and sika have a similar diet and also like mast (acorns, beech, sweet chestnut), fruit (crab apples, rosehips, blackberries, bilberries), brambles and briars, ivy and mosses. Muntjac will graze but usually browse on brambles, ivy and tree seedlings and also like fruit and mast. Water deer live mainly on grass but are developing quite a taste for vegetables and root crops. Roe are browsers rather than grazers: in the wild they happily chomp away on brambles, tree shoots, heather, bilberry and so on, though occasionally they will graze on grasses and herbs.

Whole books have been written about the damage that various deer can inflict on trees: they can be one of the forester's greatest nuisances and the cost of their 'vandalism' is quite staggering. In gardens, some deer are notorious for their love of rosebuds and shoots: roe are expert rose pruners, waiting until just before your buds are about to flower. They don't actually harm the plant; it will flower very well but rather later than you had hoped.

The trouble is that, when you first find deer in your garden, you feel immensely privileged and take great joy in watching them. And you feel the same the second time, and the third, until you begin to realise that they've had you for a sucker and are demolishing your pansies, your crocuses, your polyanthuses, your bluebell leaves and hyacinths, tulips, lilies and day lilies and water lilies, your pelargonium flowers and the wallflowers (if the rabbits didn't get them first), your sweet peas and runner beans, your windfall apples and strawberries, and especially your roses.

Some of them seem to love all yellow flowers. A roe doe regularly gives birth to her twins in my gardenside meadow and one morning I watched her, heavily pregnant, daintily selecting nothing but buttercup flowers. I thought, naïvely, that it was something to do with improving her milk for the little ones. My theory was shattered when I saw a buck doing exactly the same. In fact, the flowers are full of protein, so both sexes benefit from eating them. Nettle-tops are also selected by the lactating females of some deer species.

> *Gardens and Deer: A Guide to Damage Limitation* is a superb book by Charles Cole, devoted entirely to garden deer, which is essential and glorious reading for anybody who has a major deer problem. It is full of ingenious ideas and is written by a man who certainly knows his deer, from long experience. It even includes a comprehensive list of plants that deer do or do not eat, though they might sample them just in case. You can feel fairly safe in growing, for example, various mints, rosemary, sage, golden oregano and other herbs, primroses, mahonia, buddleia, weigela, laburnum, hypericum, cotton lavender, choisya, lavender, daffodils, lilies of the valley, peonies, woolly-leaved lamb's-ears, hellebores, daphne, oleander, rhubarb and so on.

DEER DETERRENTS

If you resent having to tailor your choice of garden plants to those that deer won't eat, there are other steps that you can take to dissuade them from using your garden as their local restaurant.

Think of it from the deer's point of view. Your garden is, if you like, an oasis: it is a treasure-trove of tastes and textures quite unlike anything deer would normally find in the wild. If the garden is also well fertilised and well watered, it is even more of an oasis, full of lush growth that no sensible deer could possibly resist. And if you have just put in a new plant or two, deer, just like rabbits, will make a beeline for it if they already habitually come into the garden: if it's new, it draws attention to itself and must be investigated, which usually means it must be tasted, nibbled and possibly even pulled out of the ground just because it's there. You could try the small-scale approach of protecting individual plants with netting or cages, or cocooning new saplings with tree guards, until the excitement of their newness has worn off and they are anyway growing strongly enough to fight for themselves and survive the occasional nibble.

One of the big problems with garden deer is that what works against one deer, or in one garden, might not work in against all deer or another garden. While a friend might swear by their own type of deterrent, you might find it worse than useless. You might also find that, although their habits are similar, your deterrent against deer doesn't work against the rabbits, and vice versa. But you do relish a challenge, don't you?

Barriers

Really, the only answer, if you positively cannot live with your deer, is to fence them out. It will cost a lot and look horrible when it is new and bare, but it might help. Deer are superb leapers and even a muntjac has been known to swarm over a 1.8m (6ft) fence. Foresters would recommend anything up to 2m (6½ft) high if red deer are about, or 1.9m (6¼ft) for roe. It needs to be good strong wire netting designed to keep out deer, not just chicken wire (for the sake of the deer, which can get in a horrible tangle with the stuff), and must be installed with proper attention to tensioning, ground-levelling and so on. Seek advice from your local forester. Properly designed, it could keep out the rabbits as well – not to mention badgers, foxes and anything else that can't fly, which might be a shame.

Electric fences are used by some but the deer have an uncanny instinct for knowing when the battery is flat or the current is off. Anyway, they'll probably jump clean over it so that they never realise it is electric; and it seems that they are far less 'shockable' than your average cow. But it might work.

Alternatively, you could grow a good hedge. The principle here is that deer don't like to jump over something if they can't see what's on the other side, so a really dense and wide hedge, with plenty of thorny and evergreen species mixed in, need be only a metre (yard) high to put off the deer. The problem, if starting from scratch, is how to protect the hedge settings from the deer until the hedge is thick enough to do the job.

I have tried a cheap option around my vegetable patch, already netted against rabbits (much too low to keep out the deer): I simply ran two almost invisible lines of fine green garden wire at about 1.2 and 1.5m (4 and 5ft) above the netting. The theory was that if a deer tried to hop over the netting, it would fail to see the green wire and would get such a surprise that it wouldn't try again. If it did see the wires, it would decide that leaping between them was too much trouble. This option actually worked for me (but it is by no means infallible – perhaps my deer were spoilt for choice elsewhere and didn't bother) and can also be used above an existing garden boundary. Perhaps you could combine it with visual deterrents like tinfoil strips bouncing in the wind.

Another simple trick, depending on what else uses your garden (including pets), is to lay large-mesh green garden netting as a loose carpet near precious plants. Deer don't like getting themselves entangled and some have the sense to avoid walking over such netting. But remember not only that they can leap well, but that the netting could trap an innocent hedgehog.

Smellies

Various deterrents based on smell are available. They are usually tar-based and the same as those you might try against rabbits and other garden raiders, with the same potential disadvantages (that they stink you out as well, they might need renewing after every splash of rain, and might not work anyway, and some are no longer allowed to be used against 'pests' without an official permit). There is always 'zoo poo', or you might try highly scented soap. There are endless helpful hints about sprinkling human urine or hanging bags of unwashed human or dog hair around the periphery of your vegetable patch or flower beds (I'm not quite sure why this should work, as there is plenty of human smell in the garden anyway). You could try hanging up mothballs, or use raw eggs or ginger or curry powder; you could try pig slurry or, in desperation, spread around the blood of a freshly killed deer as a warning to the rest of them.

Visuals and audibles

Perhaps it should be something more visual. Although unconcerned about floodlights (they quickly become used to them), deer don't like lights that keep flashing or moving erratically. It is also sometimes said that they can be startled into insecurity by other things that flash and move – for example, strips of dancing tinfoil or little mirrors swinging freely – or things that rustle at the same time (like crinkly white thin-plastic bags), or home-made scarecrows of various kinds. Then there are ultrasonic devices against all sorts of 'pests' but they may or may not be effective; you have to make sure that the deer don't get used to them, so you need to vary where they are placed and the frequencies that they emit. Even the recorded sound of howling wolves is something deer can tolerate once they've heard it a few times. Another possible noise deterrent is lines of humming wire, also used against bird raids, but individual deer might just hum along with them.

So many of the proposed deterrents simply make your beautiful garden look ugly, or get up your nose or irritate your ears. Some people try other animals as deterrents. Dogs are pretty useless, it turns out; and the theory that sheep or cows make deer uneasy is rubbish in my own experience – my garden is surrounded by livestock and the deer take no notice of them whatsoever. Llamas might do the trick.

ENOUGH!

Deer numbers have grown considerably in recent years, much to the joy of those who love to see them about the place. Others are determined to fight against nature rather than to learn to live with it, understand it, welcome it and use cunning to achieve harmony. For the fighters, this generally means killing, which must be by rifle and must be done professionally if at all. I was deeply shocked when a group of local landowners decided that the roe were out of control and should be culled. Some of the local gardeners agreed with them. Well, there's culling and there's mass slaughter. Soon they were boasting that the stalkers had shot more than a hundred. Of course, if you go down that road you have to continue because, as ever, if the habitat is attractive enough, more of the same species will move into it almost immediately. Deer are great roamers.

The cull could have been worse. Living next to a thousand acres of woodland in the 'seventies, I quite often came across maimed deer left by poachers who were using silent crossbows and dogs; the worst was a doe paralysed by injury to her spine and lying there utterly helpless, left to die slowly. I have found deer caught by the leg in snares set for foxes, screaming in terror. I have found deer in my garden seeking refuge after being mis-shot by some cack-handed warrior – a doe with a deep wound in her flank and a buck that had a broken leg reeking of gangrene from a shotgun wound. If you have ever looked into the eyes of a wounded deer, you will rage against the human assumption of the right to kill an animal for being a 'pest'.

The Squirrel Challenge

Squirrels: you either love them or loathe them. In gardens, some people welcome squirrels with open arms, charmed by their intelligence, vivacity, sheer determination and ingenuity in getting what they want. Others are driven wild by their raids on the bird nuts or their destructive invasion of loft spaces.

Even their enemies must admit that they are a delight to watch: they are full of character, full of energy, full of busy-ness, living at high speed, bounding across the lawn, twitching their agitated tails and chattering in anger or alarm, chasing each other at jerky speed up a tree, and having the winsome ability to seem more two-legged than four, using their forepaws with great dexterity to hold and manipulate their food. Some people do all they can to encourage squirrels into the garden, deliberately putting out food for them.

Others, preferring to feed wild birds, are dismayed at squirrel raids on the peanuts and are sometimes driven to wild extremes of anti-squirrel tactics. My father, in his retirement, spent much of his time and energy lying in wait for the squirrels, arming himself with the most powerful water pistol he could find and taking up his position at a bedroom window with a clear view of the bird feeder. But squirrels are too wily. They would get drenched and scamper away, only to hide round the corner and launch another raid soon after, time and time again, until my father gave up the unequal struggle.

Some people discriminate: red squirrels are 'pretty', native and under threat of extinction in Britain, while grey squirrels are 'no more than tree rats', alien invading bullies on the rampage. Very few people seem to prefer the grey to the red 'squirrel nutkin' of their childhood story books, which may have a lot to do with the perception that the grey is chasing the red right out of the country. Overpaid (in food), oversexed (some males are fecund in most months of the year, and females might be pregnant at any time from about January to July) and very definitely over here – an American import that has spread faster and further since the first pair were released in Cheshire in 1876 than it had any right to do.

Whether red or grey, each is a true tree squirrel, closely related and of the same genus, *Sciurus*. Both are indeed rodents. The red is smaller than the grey and also tends to live in coniferous forests, while the grey seems to prefer deciduous or mixed woodland, especially if it includes oak, and also beech, hazel or sweet chestnut. Greys are equally at home in urban parks, gardens and hedgerow trees, and the typical home territory of a male is about 1.5 hectares (3¾ acres).

Some greys grow coats with a suspiciously foxy tinge to them and red-backed greys are seen in some parts of the country, fooling the unwary into thinking that red squirrels have returned. Colour apart, the most obvious features of the true red are its ear tufts, though these might not be very apparent in summer.

ALL IN A DAY'S WORK

Squirrels always seem to be living life at the double. They can reach speeds of up to 29kph (18mph) on the ground, bounding along with leaps of up to 2m (6½ft) apart, and of course in trees they are in their element, dramatically acrobatic, with plenty of high-speed chasing and chattering, alternating with games of hide-and-seek. The body language of a squirrel is complex and relates to their hierarchical social structure. You can spend hours watching their antics and seeing a wide range of postures – that bushy tail is a very useful semaphore flag. They can also swim, if they must.

Their sense of smell is excellent, and much relied upon in the search for food. Their hearing is not outstanding, despite the wide range of vocalisations that they use – the low 'took took', impatient screams and the shrill, far-reaching 'chuck-chuck-chureee' as they scold each other in the tree tops or become agitated about something. Less often you might hear teeth-clacking noises or little moans. As for their eyesight, they have exceptionally sharp focusing power but also excellent wide-angle vision, although they are pretty hopeless at differentiating between colours.

Squirrels are day creatures and are early risers, often up and about before the sun rises and rushing around full of jerky energy for the next four or five hours, with another surge of enthusiasm as the day wanes towards dusk. As night falls, they are already tucked up in their dreys – round mounds of leaf material (rather tidier for reds than for greys) high in a tree – or in a tree-hole den. They also make summer resting decks out of twigs and leaves. In winter they tend to rise at dawn as usual but spend only two or three hours being active, before returning to the comfort of their winter quarters. In theory, that should mean it is safe to put out your birdfood after mid-morning if you want to avoid squirrel raids.

Squirrels do not hibernate, though they do plump themselves up enough before winter just in case the weather is too rough for them to get out and about for a couple of days (at most) and find some of those goodies that they stored during the autumn bonanza. Gardeners who discover oak and hazel seedlings sprouting in the middle of the vegetable patch or lawn probably have squirrels to thank for the bonus of free new trees.

Making babies

The drey is a nest for babies as well as somewhere to keep warm in winter. Males usually only give it a rest from about August to October in Britain; females are polyoestrous but are usually not 'in season' from September to December. Squirrels are polygamous and the 'courtship' involves a great deal of chasing and scolding and displaying. In Britain, the peak periods for births are January to March and again in May to July, depending on food supplies and weather. Most mature females have two litters a year. The gestation period is between 36 and 45 days and the litter is anything from one to seven babies but usually about three. They are born blind, deaf and naked in a well-insulated breeding drey and are suckled by a very attentive mother for seven to ten weeks. She continues to protect them after they are weaned. The more precocious youngsters can breed as young as six months.

Grub

Squirrels mainly eat grains, seeds and green food. In autumn they feast on tree mast, especially beech nuts, acorns, hazel nuts and sweet chestnuts (the average squirrel needs 60 to 80g, or 2 to 2¾oz, of mast a day), burying surplus nuts just below the soil surface or storing them in safe caches in a tree. During the year they eat assorted berries, seeds, leaves, roots, fungi, walnuts, bulbs, tubers, young shoots, galls, bark sap and catkin pollen in due season. They relish the multifaceted larders of elm, maple, sycamore and hornbeam trees, which supply them with buds, tender shoots, leaves, sappy titbits and seeds. In coniferous areas squirrels go for the cones of larches and pines, from which they can extract seeds and pollen. Occasionally a squirrel will help itself to a bird's egg or two (and maybe even a nestling) and a few insects. Most of its liquid intake comes from its food but a squirrel will also lap dew to assuage any thirst and might seek out a proper source of water in hot weather.

EVIDENCE

Evidence of squirrels – apart from seeing and hearing them – includes droppings, tracks, smells, dreys and damage.

- The **droppings** vary. They are larger than a rat's but smaller than a rabbit's (about 8mm or ⅜in diameter), round to cylindrical, often black, and are scattered about (unlike rabbits, who tend to leave their pellets in groups).
- The **tracks** usually show claw prints as well as pads, with five on the hind feet and four on the front feet, each foot

print being about 3cm (1¼in) wide. In softer ground a skidded hind print looks remarkably like a human hand, complete with thumb.

- The **trail** shows the feet grouped usually side by side, not overlapping, with the hind prints in front and clear of the front prints, then a gap in between for the hop – usually about a metre (yard) or two, or maybe half a metre if the squirrel is pottering about.
- **Bark gnawings** on the lower trunks and branches of trees are often scent-marked with urine just below the gnawed patch – you can hardly miss the rat-like smell.
- **Bark strippings** are left in shreds at the base of the tree.
- **Scratch marks** and trails on the bark might be seen on trees, especially those that support a drey.
- **Food remains**, such as fragments of nuts, berries and rosehips, might be found under a favourite feeding station on a branch or stump. Nut burials are shallow (2 to 5cm, or an inch or two), just beneath the grass or in the soil.
- **Nuts** are usually split in half lengthways to extract the kernel, or there might be a large clean-cut hole at one end. **Cones** are stripped out. **Tree shoots** are neatly cut.

Squirrels on the rampage

One of their most destructive habits is stripping or gnawing bark from trees. Sometimes this is to reach the sappy substance under the bark for food but more often it is either a social signal or to collect drey material. Trees are often killed outright by being 'ring-barked' in this way, or at the very least are laid open to invasion by disease. In conifer woods you might find long twists of stripped bark lying on the forest floor or still half-hanging on the tree trunks. Other trees are decimated by squirrels chewing their buds and young shoots.

In forestry, the squirrel is a major pest and is often ruthlessly controlled. Orchard owners and fruit growers also have problems with squirrels, both for bark stripping and for damaging the fruit. In the garden, squirrels will dig up your bulbs, tip over insecure dustbins, rootle in the lawn, eat your fruit and persistently steal food put out for the birds. In the home, the damage is more serious: a squirrel in a roof space will tear up roof insulation as desirable nesting material, exercise its teeth on the joists and even chew electric cables, which has in some cases led to the outbreak of fire.

TACTICS

Although doughty opponents, squirrels do have a few natural predators. Stoats occasionally take young squirrels from the drey (they are expert climbers). Foxes, dogs and cats will chase a squirrel on the ground but need to be skilled ratters to deal with them. Squirrels also fight each other, sometimes to the death. Some squirrels die in forest fires, or when a storm brings their tree crashing to the ground; a few might drown in floods. The biggest natural killer is starvation: despite the old wives' tale that squirrels get very fat and then hibernate all winter, in fact they cannot go for more than two or three days without food, especially when they have been weakened by the host of parasites that seem to infest most squirrels (they always seem to be alive with fleas). The squirrel's greatest enemy, however, is a human being, whether as a deliberate predator or as a motorist.

Bird lovers devise all sorts of ingenious impediments to squirrels on their way to the peanuts – things that taste nasty to squirrels but not to birds, or things that tip the animals off as soon as they land on the nuts, or spin them round to make them dizzy, or make a loud noise, or are covered with something too slippery for a squirrel to get a grip. Squirrels quickly become used to new gadgets and are so agile that they land for only a fleeting moment on each obstacle, leaping to the next perch before the ingenious device has a chance to be effective. Whole television programmes have been devoted to an obstacle course for squirrels and, in the end, the squirrels always work it out and win. It is almost as if they enjoy the challenge and would not bother if it were easy.

In theory, squirrels cannot fly, though they seem to try and are quite capable of taking a flying leap that would be beyond the scope of an Olympic long-jumper. In theory, it should be possible to devise something that a nut-raiding squirrel can neither jump nor climb up or down to. Bird-feeding stations should be far enough from any possible squirrel springboards, from the sides, above or beneath. A bird table needs to be on an unclimbable pole (which also keeps cats and foxes off the table); it can be made slippery with Vaseline or something similar, and given an inverted cone-shaped collar that prevents the squirrel from coming up-and-under.

A suspended birdfood hanger is no problem for a squirrel: the animal simply pulls up the string or chain hand-over-fist until the food is in reach, like a fisherman pulling in his nets. I used to suspend my bird feeders a long way from anything climbable on a horizontal length of very thin garden wire, far too high off the ground for a squirrel to jump up, and would then watch with amazement and awe as they did hand-over-hand scrambles all the way to the prize, just like the SAS. I had to be impressed at such skill and still cannot figure out how they managed to find any purchase on such thin wire over such long distances. My squirrel problems were finally solved by chance when a huge century-old American red oak in the copse at the top of the garden, a favourite drey-tree for squirrels, suddenly keeled over one calm January day and crashed to the ground, flattening a newly laid hazel hedge. Double whammy for the squirrels: no drey home, and no nice line of nut-producing hazel trees to lure them further into the garden.

Did they but know it, peanuts are not that good for squirrels. They would do far better sticking to hazel nuts, acorns, beechmast and sweet chestnut. Luckily, they do not remember all the ones they bury and I have managed to raise a whole new hedgerow from squirrel nuts buried in my vegetable patch.

Squirrels can become very possessive about their feeding patch in the garden. Birds keep well clear of an invading squirrel, and if another squirrel should try to join in, there is likely to be squabble. Squirrels have also been known to defy the resident dog or cat from 'their' forage area, and any dog or cat that has ever tried to catch a squirrel will know to its cost that it has to be an instant kill or it could get badly bitten, probably on its tender little nose. A cornered squirrel is always dangerous, even to humans. A determined squirrel also seems to have no fear of angry humans: I have tried chasing them off at close quarters, and have even been close enough to poke them with a bamboo pole, to very little effect. The only time they were really worried was when a cat was waiting under the rose pergola that they habitually used as a route to the bird nuts: the sound of agitation was almost heart-rending. Nor were they too happy when a bird alarm call went out as a sparrow hawk did one of its regular fly-throughs, and they were even more worried when the birds spotted a buzzard way, way up in the blue.

It is more than the birdfood problem, of course. Squirrels strip bark from garden trees as well as forest ones but in the garden it is probably because your birdfood is attracting too many squirrels. They don't seem to like each other that much and a crowd of two or more leads to social pressure. So they take it out on the trees, rather like a couple of dogs who have been posturing as if squaring up for a fight but decide to back off without losing face and promptly either cock a leg or give the ground a good scratch, flinging sods backwards. Or a cat, to save embarrassment, pretends all it really wanted was to give itself a good wash – typical displacement behaviour, which is also seen in squirrels, who might take to vigorous self-grooming after a confrontation with a rival or, if it's handy, will strip that bark off that tree.

Then there is the digging. Naturally they will dig little holes in your lawn and flower beds to bury their nuts and will dig all over the place later in the season to retrieve them. The digging, being so shallow, doesn't do much damage but they will also dig up your delicious newly planted spring bulbs. There is not a great deal you can do to stop that, but it might be worth burying a wire-netting barrier under the turf after you have planted the bulbs. In some years squirrels ignore bulbs; in others they develop a taste for them, or just dig them up because that is what squirrels do.

Apart from devising or buying anti-squirrel devices for peanut feeders (these are numerous in birdfood catalogues and pet shops), you can try spraying coyote urine about the garden – it is said to scare off squirrels, but it will get right up your nose too. The main practical weapon is to make your garden less attractive to squirrels in the first place. Even if your bird-nut feeder is irresistible, any squirrel is happier moving about in branches and is more hesitant on the ground, so you need plenty of empty lawn space between the feeder and any trees and shrubs (or rose pergolas). A new squirrel will not know about the peanuts unless it has been lured into the garden – for example, by spotting a hazel bush in full nut. Deprive the squirrels of natural food sources and of places in which to build their dreys: they will not travel huge distances to invade your peanuts.

In theory (but squirrels always defy theories) it is possible to inhibit squirrel reproduction, much as in theory you can deter or prevent rabbits and rats from having offspring. In theory, too, you can live-trap squirrels in tailor-made cages but this is far from advisable. For a start, squirrels go absolutely berserk in a cage, charging about and flinging themselves from one side to another, damaging themselves in the attempt to escape or hide, and quite possibly dying of shock from fear; the risk of death from 'trap stress' is quite high. Secondly, a grey squirrel is still not classified as a 'native' species in Britain, and it is illegal to keep one in captivity or to release it elsewhere unless you have an appropriate licence. If a squirrel *is* released elsewhere, it will probably return to its old stamping-ground even if it is as much as 2km (1¼ miles) away. In alien territory it is unlikely to last long: it will be chased off by resident squirrels and will probably start travelling immediately, running the all-too-common risk of being run over on unfamiliar roads. All of which is to say that if you live-trap a squirrel, you will probably have to kill it. And you might be killing your more tolerant neighbour's favourite squirrel.

HOME RAIDERS

The indoor squirrel is a more serious problem and its means of entry can be quite ingenious – down the chimney, for example (you need to put a very strong, unchewable guard over vulnerable chimneys). My parents lived in a very old cottage, with numerous high access points for starlings, rodents and squirrels. There was even a squirrel drey in the roof at one time (nice and dry for the little ones). You always knew when there was a squirrel in the loft because it sounded like the proverbial herd of elephants. You could become used to that, but far more dangerous were the squirrelly attempts to cut their teeth on electric cables in the roof space. Lights have been fused, squirrels have fried and fires have been started by cable-chewing, especially in cottages with thatched roofs. The indoor squirrel needs serious attention and this really is a case for calling in the experts, who will probably trap, poison or even electrically zap the culprit. A squirrel, when cornered indoors, has a very vicious bite.

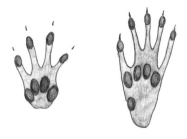

Squirrel's front and hind footprints

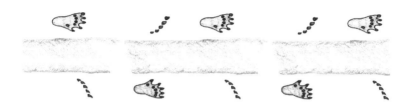

Molehills and Mountains

The mole epitomises the 'pest' dilemma and it is probably true to say that more gardeners become apoplectic about moles than about any other garden nuisance. Perhaps it is the feeling of being undermined, both physically and psychologically.

People have been moved to extreme measures: many resort to patrolling at dawn armed with a shotgun and I know of one man who eventually hired a rotavator and furiously ploughed up the whole of his once elegant lawn in frustration at the 'little gentleman in black velvet'. The lawn looked far worse as a ploughed field than it had as a patch of green studded with brown molehills, but it allowed the gardener to vent his rage and he continued to rotavate the area at monthly intervals for a year. There, he thought to himself with grim satisfaction, that'll fix the little devils! Wrong, of course. His garden was surrounded by fields. As soon as he'd relaxed his guard, the prime territory of his ex-lawn was instantly invaded again by new tenants.

And that is how it is with moles. They are highly territorial but if a territory is vacated because the resident mole has been killed or died of natural causes, then it's up for grabs and in no time at all another mole moves in. As long as the territory remains attractive as a source of food, it will be occupied. It is the very persistence of moles that so infuriates their unwitting landlords – especially, it seems, men. Perhaps it is a power thing and the insult of being bested by a small, almost blind and usually unseen enemy whose only real crime is its ignorance of the human territorial instinct. As far as the mole is concerned, the land 'belongs' to the brave; that is, to the mole who makes it his or her own.

To tackle a mole 'problem', you need to know about a mole's daily life and why it makes those heaps and furrows in your garden. Once you come to know this particular 'enemy', you will, albeit grudgingly, have to admit considerable admiration for it – you might even learn to live with moles.

KNOW THINE ENEMY

Moles are rarely seen, except in traps, but they do run above ground now and then and it is something of a surprise to discover just how small they are. The tunnel-shaped body is somewhere around 11 to 16cm (4 to 6in) long, including the head; even the biggest mole is less than the length of most people's hands, and it weighs less than half a pack of butter. And this is the threatening creature that moves mountains . . .

The dark coat of a mole is rather handsome and thoroughly practical: the fur, like velvet, has a raised nap so that the mole can move backwards or forwards in a close-fitting tunnel without getting ruffled. Somewhere in that fur

are two tiny eyes, usually hidden from an observer but functional, though the eyesight is poor. Its senses of hearing and smell are good but most important of all is its sense of touch, particularly the vibrissae (hairs) on its snout, which are highly sensitive to the slightest vibration in the ground – be it from a tumbling worm or the distant tread of an approaching gardener. Its snout is also very sensitive to changes in humidity and temperature.

Moles are solitary animals and there is only one per tunnel system, which may surprise those who assume from the number of molehills in their garden that an army of tunnellers is at work. More molehills often means too few worms (so the mole needs to go searching) or, especially around February, just more activity – not more moles. They are highly aggressive to each other and will not tolerate another mole within their home range, the size of which depends on the food-richness of the environment. For example, in grassland, you might find up to eight moles per hectare (2½ acres) in winter but twice that number in summer, when the living is easier. Old pasture is a very happy hunting ground for a mole (and what is lawn but old pasture?): it is rich with food and is normally undisturbed by cultivation. Some moles seem to specialise in pasture; others prefer woodland, but the aim is the same – to find a territory that is easy to work (but not so easy that tunnels collapse), with plenty of food and not belonging to another mole.

Mole meal

As its underground lifestyle implies, moles live on animals found in the soil. In winter, earthworms are top of the list; in summer or dry weather the balance swings to various insects, especially the larvae of beetles and flies. Slugs and snails, millipedes, cockchafers (maybug grubs) and even carrion are also eaten. Sometimes you will find a mole's worm larder: it deliberately damages the worms (usually by chomping the head end) so that they are more or less immobilised but still alive and then piles them together in or near the nest so that it can snack on fresh worms at will. A mole eats the equivalent of about half its own body weight of food a day – perhaps 40 to 50g (1½ to 1¾oz).

The tunnel system is crucial to food-finding; in fact, the tunnels act as traps. Earthworms, for example, tend to migrate through the soil on a regular basis: in the evening they work their way up to the surface to feed and perhaps mate, and just before dawn they work their way down again. As they do so, they tumble into the tunnel and take the easy option of wriggling along it – straight into the jaws of an alert early-bird mole. Various larvae are equally regular in their up-and-down migrations.

A day in the life of . . .

Moles seem to have regular habits. They are active by night as well as by day (not much difference if you are underground) and usually work almost continuously for about four and a half hours and then retire to the nest for three and a half hours, repeating the cycle throughout a 24-hour period. You will often find that all the local moles are active or resting at the same time as each other. Sometimes they take a quick nap in the middle of an active period, simply downing tools and napping wherever they happen to be in the tunnel system. For more serious resting, they retire to the nest.

Dawn is an important time for moles to be wide awake, as the earthworms are on that daily migration. Patrolling is constant, not only to catch the worms but also to keep the tunnel system in good repair and sometimes to dig in search of other food, such as grubs. Occasionally a mole will come above ground for food, especially after a shower of rain during an otherwise dry period – provided it has plenty of cover so that it can avoid predators. Sometimes it will come to the surface in search of nesting material, such as grass and leaves. The young have to come above ground in due course to disperse and find their own territories, and they are at that stage highly vulnerable to tawny owls, buzzards, herons, weasels, foxes, cats and occasionally dogs. Cats, dogs and foxes seem to catch moles simply because they can – they often don't bother to eat them.

Going underground

A good territory, then, has not only the food supply but also the right kind of soil for tunnelling. Moles avoid stony soils; they also avoid very shallow soils, as these are lacking in food, or very acid soils such as heather moorland and coniferous forests. They can manage in heavy, wet soils but not those that are always waterlogged.

Moles are excellent swimmers, incidentally, and can often be seen in flooded meadows paddling a hasty retreat until the floods subside. Water is important to them and it is said that they can detect a source of water more than a kilometre (½ mile) away; sometimes several moles, despite their mutual antipathy, will use a communal tunnel to a good water supply. They will drink dew if they can't find a more abundant source.

The tunnel system is a work of great engineering skill and represents a huge amount of labour: one mole is capable of shifting 6kg (13lb) of soil in 20 minutes, a rate that could create a pretty large tunnel system all in one go. The system is adapted to the soil type. For example, it will be extensive in stony, shallow soils but mainly on just one level. In older pasture the tunnels are usually at several levels, ranging from shallow foraging runs to deep permanent tunnels perhaps 70 or even 100cm (2 or 3ft) down into the soil. The system is elaborate, with tunnels branching here, there and everywhere, and moles seem to have a perfect mental image of the layout, always knowing exactly where they are in the system.

When a mole first colonises a new territory, it must quickly create escape routes, locate food sources and check out where the neighbours are. To this end, it digs very shallow tunnels just below the surface, in the root zone: in grassland these can be seen as slightly humped runs under the grass, usually without breaking the surface (though sometimes these foraging tunnels cave in); or in newly cultivated ground you might make out a slight ridge in the soil. In making these shallow runs, the mole pushes the loosened soil upwards as it goes along, leaving a continuous line.

For a while at this stage the new mole has no proper nest; it just makes a side-chamber in the tunnel. Once it has the area sussed, however, it begins to dig a deeper system of tunnels and this is when molehills begin to appear. Molehills are the soil excavated from the deeper tunnel system by the mole's massive front paws: it pushes the loosened soil up a more or less vertical shaft to the surface. Thus new molehills often indicate a new mole at work, or an existing mole renovating its tunnel system. Once a system has been built, a mole (left undisturbed) will use it for the rest of its life, simply repairing it and making any seasonal adjustments when necessary. For example, in very cold or very dry weather it might have to tunnel even deeper to follow its food down into the soil. In the brief mating season, a male might make a determined, long straight tunnel or 'courtship run' directly into a female's territory.

Every now and then you might find an extra-large molehill or 'fortress', sometimes as much as a metre high and generally riddled with tunnels. Often you will find a nest somewhere within or under the fortress, but a mole does not have to build a fortress for its nest. Usually the nest (generally only one per system) is simply built into a chamber to one side of a main tunnel and lined with whatever materials are available nearby. The nest is the bedroom, somewhere safe and warm for sleeping and resting, and may also be a nursery for the young.

Mole mates

Reproduction must be a dilemma for a mole, by nature aggressive towards all other moles of whatever sex. The very short mating season starts in March in most of Britain and it's a fairly frantic time. Females are willing and able to mate for perhaps only three or four days in that season, and a male virtually takes his life in his paws: if he dared to invade a female's territory on a day when she was not ready to mate, he'd meet with a very rough reception indeed. To make sure of perpetuating his genes, a male mole mates with as many females as he can find. This is when he is at his most vulnerable, not just to female moles but also to being trapped or caught by predators – he's out of his own territory and isn't really concentrating anyway.

The four or so babies are born after a four-week gestation and are suckled for about a month. At six weeks they are beginning to find their own food and at only two months old they are being made unwelcome at home and start to look for their own territories. They will not, however, be capable of breeding until they are about a year old. Some females manage two litters a year in a good season but in Britain most have only one.

LET'S HEAR IT FOR THE MOLE!

Moles do indeed inflict superficial damage in gardens by leaving their spoil heaps all over the lawn, though wise gardeners make use of their tilling by exploiting the nicely sifted soil for seedbeds. Their tunnelling does, it must be admitted, sometimes cause loss of plants when the mole-run is immediately under a new shrub or row of seedlings (in which case the mole was probably doing you a favour by trawling for root-eating larvae), leaving the roots dangling in mid-air.

The tunnels also serve as (literally) mole-drains through the soil. An old friend of mine, Bert Winchester, was a gamekeeper many years ago on a large country estate. One day he was summoned by Lord X to deal with a plague of moles defacing the stately parkland. 'Get rid of the damned things, Winchester!' demanded his Lordship. Bert, a born naturalist who knows a great deal about wildlife and about how the environment works, queried the wisdom of this but his Lordship insisted and so Bert dutifully set about laying traps and ridding the park of moles. A year later, his Lordship remarked with alarm that the park was flooding, which it had never done before. Of course it is, Bert told him, the moles aren't draining it for you any more.

In the early part of the nineteenth century Mr J Baxter of Lewes produced his splendid *Library of Agricultural and Horticultural Knowledge*. In the section on 'Vermin', he wrote: 'Moles are by some agriculturists considered as extremely mischievous. They believe that by throwing up the mould upon the surface, they prove of the greatest injury to the land, and in some cases where they are very numerous, render it utterly useless. Others, however, of the first-rate experience, have argued warmly in defence of the moles, which have, according to their views, been so unjustly condemned to the trap. Among these we have the Ettrick Shepherd, who goes so far as to call his friend, the moles – "the blessed and innocent little pioneers." The foundation of Mr. Hogg's argument is, that they annually give the first top-dressing to our pasture lands, and that too more regularly and effectually than man.'

You can therefore decide to make the most of molehills on the lawn by spreading the heaps about with a rake to act as the grass's top-dressing. That's a nice positive thought. Further, according to the said Mr Hogg, it seemed that in some parts of Scotland many of the 'smaller proprietors of land' actually begged their laird to stop employing mole-catchers and 'to spare the remnant of their old friends, and suffer them to breed again', because the livestock had been reduced since the destruction of moles by 'at least one-sixth, and in some instances one-fifth; and not only that, but has introduced two exterminating diseases, the pining and the foot-root, neither of which was known in that district till the extermination of the moles.'

TRIAL AND SENTENCE

A molehill is evidence enough for most people that a mole is active in their garden. For what it's worth, the track is quite unusual: the print of the forefoot is a line of four claw marks running from front to back on the outside of the foot rather than from side to side, and the five claw marks on the hindfoot form an inverted L-shape. You are unlikely to find any droppings or to hear a mole's voice unless it is being attacked, when it will give one loud squeak. Otherwise an excited mole might twitter, but it is barely audible to humans.

Deterrents

Acting on the principle that another mole will move into the territory as soon as you ruthlessly cull the current resident – and will probably do so within 24 hours and then start digging afresh to make its mark, so to speak – it is better by far to learn to live with moles and admire their engineering skills, strength, energy and diligent persistence. Call a truce. Accept that the mole has just as much right to be there as you do, and probably more, as for a mole it is a matter of life and death. A smallish garden is usually home to only a single mole but others are always lurking across the boundaries and so, unless you exterminate every mole for miles around, you won't win.

As already explained, most moles will throw up new heaps only if you disturb existing heaps and dislodge soil into the tunnels, or seasonally when either food is scarce (in which case the mole is tunnelling deeper and is doing you a favour by improving the garden's drainage) or the young are dispersing and setting up their own territories. Once the basic tunnel system is established, there should be very little provocation in terms of molehills, and your mole is likely to reside in it for the rest of its life – usually at least two years or, if its teeth hold out, as much as five years or more, which is long enough to earn it a pet name.

The first question is why the mole finds your garden so attractive anyway and, if it seems feasible, how to reduce that attraction. This is unlikely to be a sensible project, if you look at it holistically. There is very little point in trying to eradicate the mole's food supply: earthworms in particular are vital to the health of the garden. Constant cultivation to disturb a mole and push its patience beyond the limit is practicable only in the vegetable patch.

So, what can you do about an existing rash of molehills that offends your aesthetic senses and clogs up the mower? First of all, in a lawn, the soil in the heap will be covering a small patch of grass and needs to be removed as soon as possible, before it smothers the growth of the grass and allows 'wasteland' weeds to invade the bare soil. Under the heap, the grass is still growing except for at the actual mouth of the excavation hole: you can generally feel a sort of raised plug at this point. In cold weather, you could try sprinkling the heaps with water last thing in the evening before a frosty night: in the morning it should be easy to lift up the entire frozen heap cleanly. Otherwise, simply shovel up the soil carefully, trying your best not to send it cascading back into the tunnel through the surprisingly small excavation hole, then gently tamp down the slight tump if your mower isn't capable of cutting without scalping. The mole will probably throw up another, smaller heap to get rid of any soil you inadvertently pushed back into its tunnel but in due course the pair of you will be in balance. Be patient.

There are countless old wives' tales of how to deter moles by making life uncomfortable for them, usually employing noises, smells or physical barriers. Baxter, in his *Library of Agricultural and Horticultural Knowledge*, suggested an alternative to trapping: 'Place slices of leek, garlic or onion in a green state within their tracts: their antipathy to these vegetables is so great, that they will immediately leave their haunts and expose themselves to be taken.' Another tip was to sprinkle coffee grounds into mole-runs, but it would take a lot of coffee to deter a dedicated mole.

Some people put something scratchy into the tunnels, like gorse clippings or threads of bramble and briar; they plant things that makes noises, like children's plastic windmills, or bottles with their necks above ground so that they catch the whistle of the wind, or those birthday cards that play endless tunes, or high-tech ultrasonic devices and vibrators. Most of these devices simply encourage the mole to tunnel even more energetically, either to go round the obstruction or to create a new network in the same territory, and the mole can probably dig more quickly and more persistently than you can plant your deterrents, which are likely to be casually heaved out of the ground by the little miner anyway.

Some people are more determined and try to drown their mole by flushing water through the system. The mole simply moves to another part of the system until the water has subsided – it's quite used to this in nature; it would only stay away if the garden was more or less permanently waterlogged or, conversely, if the soil was stony or too thin to support a decent food supply, or so sandy that tunnels simply collapsed when dug. Other people rig up a hose attached to some sort of petrol-driven engine and try to fumigate the animal, or pour down the tunnel some strong-smelling liquid such as ammonia, creosote or Renardine. This might move the mole out of that particular tunnel temporarily but it (or another mole) will return in the end.

Country people often claim that moles won't dig where spurge is growing – the milky white sap is unpleasant for humans as well as moles – but to have any effect this would mean blanketing your entire garden.

A near neighbour of mine, whose cottage is surrounded by fields and woodland, tried 'fencing' moles out: he dug down along his garden boundaries and made a barrier of stones, old corrugated iron and wire netting. Well, he didn't dig deep enough: the mole in due course dug deeper and came up smiling on the other side. You would probably need to sink your barrier as much as a metre deep, which means a lot of digging and certainly isn't worth the labour and expense.

If the situation is truly unbearable, you can call in a licensed mole-catcher armed with nasties like cyanide and strychnine. The latter is a particularly reprehensible method: strychnine-charged earthworms are dropped into the runs, but of course they can also be eaten by other small mammals

One deterrent might be to try creating a wild area that is so appealing to moles that they won't bother with the rest of the garden – full of scrummy worms near the compost heap, perhaps. Another theory that has not been tried in practice, as far as I know, is to use the smell of moles themselves. The possession of a territory is generally advertised by the scent of the resident and that scent is usually enough to keep other moles away. So, if you could somehow bottle mole-scent and make sure that an existing tunnel system was always full of it – at least towards the edges of the territory, even though no real mole was in residence – you never know, it might work for a while . . .

or birds, or the poisoned mole itself might be eaten as
carrion by an unsuspecting animal, including a dog. Older
and more patient mole-catchers set careful traps, and this
does require skill: although a well-placed trap may catch its
victim, many a mole simply tunnels its way around the trap
and thumbs its nose at you, especially if the trap smells of
humans. Trapping is labour-intensive as well as requiring
skill and, again, a new mole will come into the system very
soon. This also applies, of course, in the case of blasting a
moving molehill with a shotgun or whanging down on it
with the back of a spade to stun the mole, flick him out and
dispose of him somehow or other.

Foxed

Perhaps no wild animal in Britain evokes such mixed emotions as the fox, which is now almost more common in cities than in the countryside. It is supremely versatile: it can eat just about anything and live just about anywhere, adapting to circumstances and making the most of any situation. Even those who hunt it from the safety of horseback behind a pack of hounds admire the fox, which is perhaps why they hunt it. One huntsman I knew wrote a delightful little book about Charlie Fox, trying to tell the story from the fox's point of view but still claiming that the fox 'enjoyed' being hunted. Another particularly avid huntsman, who wanted to call his memoirs 'Nimrod' (he had also been a big-game hunter), did his best to persuade me that those who rode to hounds were ardently green conservationists, but in the end he admitted that he hunted because he loved the chase – nothing whatsoever to do with conservation or even with 'pest' control.

The pest status of the fox differs according to its environment. In the country, foxes do indeed go berserk in

chicken runs and slaughter every bird in sight: they are
predators by nature and make the most of a supply that
seems to be offered on a plate as they never know when they
might next get their next meal (some mustelids are the
same). This apparently wilfully destructive act can be
heartbreaking for the chicken keeper but it is perhaps more
the fault of the humans who have confined the chickens,
gathering so much temptation into one place without
making absolutely sure that no predator can have access.
And that means you have to out-fox the fox, which requires
considerable guile and persistence to match its own. A fox
has a 'collapsible' ribcage, which allows it to squeeze
through unbelievably small gaps.

Sometimes it is claimed that rural foxes also kill lambs. In
reality, foxes tend to take the easy option and it is more
likely that they scavenge on a lamb already dead or take
advantage of one that is nearly so. They will certainly eat
afterbirth and in some circumstances some foxes may
become lamb killers.

Unfortunately for the fox, its natural prey – especially
rabbits and rodents – are also deemed to be pests and are
constantly controlled by human intervention, thus reducing
the supply available to foxes and other predators. So
perhaps it is little wonder they turn to domesticated prey
instead. It is highly unlikely that a fox will ever kill your cat:
there are countless eye-witnesses who have watched foxes
and cats in the same garden, each studiously ignoring or
avoiding the other. But pet rabbits and other small caged
mammals are a different story: from the fox's point of view,
they are natural prey.

The urban fox is more often considered a pest for raiding
dustbins and for its rather eerie vocalisations. As with other
wild animals, some people are enchanted to find that a fox
visits their garden and many will deliberately put out food

to attract foxes for the pleasure of fox-watching. Others regard them as vermin and probably accuse them of all sorts of misdemeanours that are equally likely to be the fault of cats and stray dogs.

KNOWING FOXES

Foxes do not need to be described: everyone knows, from their earliest storybook days, that a fox is like a foxy red dog with a low-held bushy tail, sharp yellow eyes (with vertical pupils), large upright ears and a long, slender snout. What comes as a surprise to those who see a fox in the flesh for the first time is just how small it is – not much bigger than a tomcat and about the same as a miniature poodle. They are only around 40cm (16in) tall at the shoulder and could walk under the belly of a friendly German shepherd dog without having to stoop. The tail is about as long as the body and a fox might measure around 110cm (3ft 8in) from the tip of its tail to the tip of its sharp muzzle. The weight of most dog (male) foxes is less than twice that of a newborn human baby, and that of vixens (females) is about 5.5kg (12lb). I've had light-footed tame foxes climbing on my back and you'd hardly know they were there (they were being cared for by Eric Ashby, the wildlife film-maker and photographer, and protector of foxes, badgers and deer in the New Forest).

In the wild, foxes have learned that humans are dangerous and so they generally prefer the cover of darkness or twilight, when their prey is also active. Although they tend to 'lie up' in a secluded spot during the day, they are also quite often seen going about their business as bold as brass in daylight as well. Being such adaptable animals, they might lie up in a den below ground, or under some brambles, or even sunbathe on a flat roof in town or take cover beneath a shed.

Foxes generally live above ground for most of the year, taking shelter when necessary under handy shrubbery or even in a tree. Sometimes they go underground, especially when there are cubs. The shape of the entrance to a den, or earth, is different from that of a badger to accommodate the shape of the animal: the mouth of a badger's sett is usually wider than it is high, and the reverse is true for a fox, whose entrance is about 25cm (10in) high and who seems to be quite happy to take over a rabbit burrow. Another difference between fox and badger earths is that the fox, especially one with cubs, often leaves old scraps of food, feathers and bones lying around outside and in, which the houseproud badger would never do.

Fox food

Foxes often bury surplus food to be eaten later, and they *do* remember where they put it. One very snowy winter I watched as a fox decided to cache half a coconut put out for the birds. Its first problem was to get a grip on this new food and eventually it thrust its lower jaw inside the shell and gripped the upper part between its teeth. Then, head held high, it trotted off with its prize and buried it in the snow in the field. Unfortunately, I never had a chance to watch how it tackled eating the coconut. The more likely food caches are birds' eggs, small mammals, chicken heads and bones (including butcher's marrow bones stolen from careless dogs). The fox has the sense to spread its hiding places over a wide area to fool any robbers.

The fox is an opportunistic omnivore and will eat a wide range of whatever is available locally. As a predator it takes rabbits, rodents (especially voles) and occasionally juvenile or injured gamebirds. Shrews or moles might be killed but are rarely eaten, and toads are shunned with distaste, but it eats earthworms and insects, fruit of many kinds and vegetables from the garden; it also scavenges on carrion, birdfood, scraps and whatever it might find in an overturned dustbin or on the compost heap. The average fox needs to eat about 500g (18oz) of food a day, which means a mind-boggling twenty voles, a hundred large earthworms or, more easily, a young rabbit.

On the right track

The typical gait of a fox is trotting, usually in a more or less straight line – in contrast to dogs, who are much less purposeful and meander about checking on this and that. The fox's pawprint is neater and more oval than a dog's, with the front two pads close together and pointing forwards. I have always been intrigued at the relationship between dogs and foxes: my own large farm-bred mongrel used to hate them with a venom for no obvious reason and I always knew when a fox had been in the garden overnight because the dog's hackles would rise as soon as he went outside in the morning; his nose would go down and he'd be off on the scent.

Trail of a dog, less tidy than a fox's in every respect.
Claw marks show that this is not a cat's trail:
cats on the move keep their claws retracted

Foxes are often betrayed by their scent and most people can catch the whiff, even if they don't recognise it. The droppings are frequently potent with the same musty smell and are long and twisted, with tapering ends. The colour of the droppings or 'castings' varies according to the fox's food: they are often black when fresh but range from dark brown to greenish-grey, and you can usually see the remains of bits of insects, prey hair (perhaps linking two droppings) and small bone fragments in them, or even blackberry pips in the autumn. Like some dogs, foxes often deposit their faeces on prominent objects such as a thistle or stone in the field, or even just a clump of grass.

Wisps of fox hair caught on a barbed-wire fence or thorny hedge are unmistakably foxy red with black and white bands. In tussocky grassland you might be able to see where the fox has been shoving its snout into the grass searching for voles, but don't be fooled: I know of a golden retriever who actually thinks he is a cat and spends hours shoving his nose into grass tussocks looking for voles, then frantically scrabbling at the grass, leaving exactly the same evidence as a fox.

Chocolate cubs

The sight of a bewildered and apparently deserted chocolate-coloured cub or two is sometimes the first evidence people have that a fox has been using their garden. Usually it is not a good idea to 'rescue' such cubs: their mother will probably come back and take them off to a safe place once nobody is around. Talk to the RSPCA for guidance (they publish some excellent leaflets) before you even think of rescuing a cub.

The mating season is obvious when there are local foxes: you cannot help but hear them, especially within a couple of hours or so of sunset. Courting foxes in winter call out with an unearthly scream or wail; they also chatter, and emit a short series of two to four high-pitched yaps at intervals as a sort of 'here I am' signal – you can often hear the route a fox is taking as the sound of the barks moves across the landscape. To some, fox noises are spooky; to some, a warning of trouble in the chicken run; but to others, they are a joy and you feel you are right out there with them. They are perhaps one of the most evocative of nocturnal countryside sounds. It is said that foxes have a range of 28 different calls, but many go unnoticed by humans.

The mating season is from about the middle of January to the end of February. The vixen comes into heat only once; she is in oestrus for about three weeks but only truly fertile for about three days, which means that the dog fox, who is fertile for considerably longer, needs to be ready and waiting. Most foxes are monogamous: they have one mate and there is one litter a year of up to perhaps eight cubs, but usually about five.

The cubs are born after 52 or 53 days in an earth that is usually built under the protection of tree roots on a well-drained site such as a bank or slope, preferably hidden by undergrowth. In urban areas, the vixen often burrows under a garden shed or finds her way under floorboards and into cellars. She will stay with the cubs without emerging for the first two days and leaves them for only very brief intervals for the first two weeks; the dog fox will bring food to her and the litter, and quite often there will be 'aunties' to help as well. The cubs make their first ventures outside when about a month old, and they are weaned within six weeks. They are enchantingly playful and it is always a delight to watch a family of cubs in the woods playing games with each other or pestering their mother by pouncing on her brush.

Sometimes the vixen moves her cubs to a new home, carrying them there one by one (which is when you are most likely to find 'deserted' cubs in your garden). By June she will often hide them during daylight in a woodpile or an outbuilding, say, or in the middle of a cereal crop or bramble patch. By the end of the summer they are fully grown and soon begin to disperse to find their own areas, sometimes involving journeys of several miles and often ending sadly in death on the roads. Although in theory a fox could live for more than eight years, few achieve as much as half of that potential lifespan.

FOX PROBLEMS?

The main gripes against foxes are that they might kill poultry and ducks, harass or kill caged pets, make strange night noises, dig under sheds and fences, scratch at or chew woodwork, rip open rubbish bags, tip over dustbins, steal birdfood, raid fruit, and leave their own scent-marks and potent smelly droppings about the place.

The attractions of your garden include food (live, fresh or scrappy) and shelter (thick shrubbery to hide in, sheds to hide under, roof gulleys to rest in and flat roofs to sunbathe peacefully on). If you don't want foxes in your garden, you can take steps to make it less attractive to them.

Firstly, make sure that it really is a fox that is causing the problems. Dustbins, for example, are equally likely to be raided by badgers, dogs, cats and even squirrels. Secondly, if the foxes are young ones, they are probably on their way to somewhere else during the dispersal time and won't stay for long. Thirdly, there is absolutely no point in destroying or removing foxes from your territory: another one will simply move in to take their place if it remains attractive. Some people are reduced to summoning fox trappers to rid them of foxes, but what happens to the trapped fox? Most people don't like the thought of it being killed and so they ask that it be released 'somewhere in the countryside'. The fox will then be in another fox family's territory and will be chased off. If it is an urban fox, it is used to easy pickings and will have a devil of a time scratching a much tougher rural living; also, many urban foxes have mange and why should you spread that among healthy country foxes? Finally, in an urban situation, 'your' foxes might be giving considerable pleasure to countless other people, and who are you to deprive them?

The answer is to make your garden unattractive. Clear out those inviting patches of brambles and nettles where a fox might take shelter in winter. Block up vacated earths (making absolutely certain there are no animals in there first) with rubble and soil. Make birdfood inaccessible by putting it too high for a fox to reach, which is higher than you might think. Put your rubbish bags in a bin and tie down the dustbin lid with bungee ropes. Put your compostables in a compost bin rather than on a heap. Concentrate any barricades on the weak points in your boundaries that foxes habitually use for access.

Don't use stinkers like creosote, which can actually harm your own pets. Renardine (see page 54) will probably repulse foxes, but it is a difficult stink to live with. Physical barriers against foxes need careful thought: foxes are excellent diggers, jumpers, climbers and swimmers and very persistent if the lure is strong enough. Any fencing would need to be at least 2m (6½ft) high, with an outward tip-over at the top to frustrate climbers and a buried outward turnover at the base to deter diggers. You could try electric fencing (either netting or with several strands of plain wire), which is a trick used by gamekeepers around pheasant pens and by ornamental-fowl owners around ponds: at least two electric fencing wires are put at about the fox's nose level, on the basis that a fox will approach the fence nose first and not like what it feels. Electric fences do not actually harm an animal: they simply give a very unpleasant sensation, especially on something as sensitive as a nose.

Alternatively, give in gracefully and enjoy the company of foxes. You will probably find that they are not half as much trouble as others have led you to believe. Salute the arch survivor and admire its beauty!

Bother with Badgers and Slinkies

You should be so lucky! Most people have never seen a live badger and not that many have seen a dead one, which is surprising in that badgers are widespread throughout Britain, except on some of the islands.

Badgers are mustelids, which means they are related to weasels, stoats, ferrets, polecats, mink, pine martens and otters. This also means they have some fairly potent musk scent glands under the tail. They are instantly recognisable: the badger is the only British mammal to have that distinctive striped face (not unlike the mask of a skunk). They are the largest of Britain's native mustelids but even so usually measure less than a metre from the tip of their long snout to their end of the short tail. The average weight of a male (boar) is about 12kg, or 26lb; a female (sow) is about 2kg, or 4½lb, less. The young are known as cubs.

The badger is one of the most highly protected animals in Britain and there are numerous laws in its favour. For example, quite apart from trying to kill a badger (unless you are licensed to do so) or to practise something obscene like badger-baiting, it is illegal even to attempt to deter badgers by using creosote, diesel oil, mothballs and so on, either by placing such substances down badger setts or by using them across regular badger routes into your property. On the other hand, there are certain repellents that rely largely on taste rather than smell, which might be usable by those whose concern is that badgers are eating their nearly-ready-for-the-table sweetcorn and carrots or digging up bulbs. There is little or no research into whether these repellents – or any others – are actually effective against badgers, which are very persistent animals once they know about a good source of food. It is also your responsibility to check whether or not you can use them legally against badgers anyway.

In trying to dissuade badgers from gracing you with their presence, you need to tread very carefully indeed. First of all, get to know about badgers – and you might then find them so interesting that you will want to encourage rather than discourage their visits.

BADGERING ABOUT

Badgers are crepuscular (twilight) and nocturnal animals, spending the day snoozing underground, which is why they are so rarely seen. They are also very alert to danger and rely heavily on their acute senses of hearing and smell; their eyesight, not surprisingly, is not much good at anything, especially at more than about 6m (20ft) away, other than being aware of movement. They do like a spot of early or late sunbathing now and then, if they are in an undisturbed neighbourhood, but normally they're sound asleep underground during the day and emerge with great caution just as the light is fading enough for your eyes to deceive you.

That's what some books will tell you. In fact I have quite often seen badgers in daylight in my own garden, especially on long summer evenings. As for their alertness to danger, it depends on circumstances. In the garden, where they particularly fancy overripe bananas on the compost heap, they couldn't care less when they see me at the window, or even when I step outside for a closer look. They ignore my torchlight after dark and don't care if I switch on a light indoors or out. I always know when the badgers have been through the garden, or along the track, as they leave a distinctive musky smell, and an even stronger one in their dug-out latrine pits near the sett or near their home-range boundaries, where you might find quite an accumulation of droppings. They don't bother to cover the droppings, which are rather like those of a dog and quite often contain remains of beetles, blackberry seeds and other titbits.

As well as evidence in the way of smells and droppings, the presence of badgers is very obvious in snow or firm mud: their track is highly distinctive. Look for a sausage-shaped pad print behind a line of five oval to round toe prints (most animal paws leave four toe prints). It is very different from the paw print of most other mammals. Another piece of evidence is a vandalised wasp nest or bee nest, dug out and ripped apart by a badger in search of the grubs and the honey. You might come across shallow scrapes, or snaffles, where a badger has been scrabbling for roots, or you might find deep scratch marks on trees or posts where a badger has been cleaning its hefty claws. Look also for its coarse black, silver and white hairs caught on barbed wire or thorny hedges.

You usually hear a badger before you can see one, probably crashing about in the undergrowth. Sometimes you hear what sounds like an old tramp coughing and grunting and snorting, but it's only a badger. Sometimes you're fooled into thinking that one of the moorhens has shouted an alarm call but, again, it is only a badger sow. Quite often you hear the screams of badgers in the early months of the year, which can be unnerving if you don't know what unearthly creature is making the noise, or you might hear a whickering or purring sound from a boar at closer quarters.

Late one afternoon I heard some squealings in the track outside my cottage and went to investigate. Two badgers were having an argument near the garden gate. I stood three or four strides away watching them, and they took no notice. Their squabble was a minor one, all talk and bluster, and they agreed to part, one going one way and the other heading in the opposite direction towards me. So oblivious was the latter to the 'danger' of my presence that he literally brushed against my legs as he passed, muttering to himself. More typically, I have often heard the snuffling of a badger in the woods in the early morning and been able to watch at close quarters (again, within a few strides) for as long as I felt like lingering. Rootling in the leafmould was far more important to the badgers than an idle human being.

A neighbour has had many an encounter with the local badgers and, again, they seem to think he is part of the scenery, even when he starts shouting with rage at their attempts to get into his chicken run or chases them off as they root out his prize-winning carrots yet again just a few days before the local horticultural show. (Every now and then you come across a rogue badger that might even take a sitting hen, but this is very rare – it's more likely that the badger is after grain put down for the hens, or perhaps wants to sneak off with an egg.) From the badgers' point of view, we humans are irrelevant and they certainly don't recognise us as providers of the very goodies that in our eyes they are pilfering but in their eyes 'harvesting from the wild'.

Badgers are powerful animals and perhaps that is why they often seem fearless; their only real enemies are humans. At a private viewing of a wildlife film, I watched as the camera rested its gaze on a fox peacefully having a good scratch on a riverside path. The camera panned away to another part of the path to catch sight of a badger ambling along it in the typically rolling and dogged badger fashion, nose down, backside sashaying like a portly matron on the catwalk. The fox continued to scratch, unaware of the approaching badger. The badger reached the fox and, without pausing, walloped him into the river with one powerful swipe of an irritable paw. The fox, bobbing in the water with a look of utter amazement on his face, didn't know what had hit him. The badger, who probably didn't even see the fox until it was virtually in touching distance, continued on its way.

At home

Badgers have a highly organised social structure, based on groups of families occupying a home range of anything up to 40 or 50 hectares (100 to 125 acres), depending on available resources.

The mating season in Britain is mainly from February to May but they can continue to mate until October. Their breeding cycle is unusual: the females do not ovulate unless stimulated to do so by copulation, and then implantation of the fertilised egg is delayed until the time is right, which might be anything from three to nine months. Eight weeks later the cubs are born, which might be any time from the end of December to the end of March, but mainly in the first half of February in southern Britain. The number of cubs ranges from one to five (usually twins or triplets) and they are born underground in the sett, where they are suckled for up to three and a half months. They start to venture above ground for the first time at perhaps eight or nine weeks old and by fifteen weeks old they are becoming quite adventurous. Badgers are playful animals, young or old, and spend a lot of their above-ground time socialising with each other.

Sows are very protective of their cubs: they will keep other badgers away from the sett, and the boar gets pushed out of the home before the cubs are even born. Female cubs are mature at about fifteen months old and males at about two years old. Given good luck and once they have passed the dangers of being young, which sometimes includes being killed by a bad-tempered old boar, badgers can live for at least fifteen years.

Badgers have very regular habits. Once they have found a suitable habitat, they stick with it. They prefer the right soil for creating a home in: diggable but not so diggable that the tunnels collapse. The perfect site is usually well drained and in woodland or a copse, probably under tree roots (which make good ceilings) or where a diggable sandy layer meets a more solid substrate that won't collapse overhead, maybe on a sheltered slope, with some protective under-growth, but close to open land such as old pasture, which makes an ample larder. But badgers are adaptable animals: you might find a sett in the middle of a field or open moorland, on a cliff or in a quarry; you might find them at home in a cave, under a building or even in an old rubbish dump. It all depends on whether local food is available and on the lack of disturbance.

The entrance to a badger's sett is distinctive: the shape of the hole fits the shape of the badger and is generally wider than it is high. There will be a large heap of excavated soil outside it, fresh when the badgers have been clearing out ready for nesting and intermingled with old bedding material (bracken, hay, grass, moss and the like). Sometimes you will find a pile of bedding apparently being put outside to air in the sun, like an old-fashioned housewife's blankets being hung out in spring. Badgers have very clean habits and a high standard of personal hygiene, but if you stand outside a sett you will probably detect their faint musk, or even see a gentle steam rising from all that underground breathing on a cold day. Incidentally, badgers do not usually hibernate, though they might go to ground for a while in bad winter weather when it is not worth wasting precious energy on searching for hard-to-find food.

Old setts can be extensive, with an elaborate system of tunnels and chambers at several levels, and with several entrances. Some go back centuries: once the badgers have found a good place, they and their descendants continue to use it for ever, unless disaster of some kind strikes – like the building of a housing estate or motorway. Even then they might try to return, which is why some owners of new houses find badgers tunnelling under the garden shed to rebuild the sett.

Humans are the main enemy, either deliberately or unwittingly. Many badgers are killed on the roads, or on electrified railway lines; the unfortunate few still fall prey to badger diggers and occasionally to hounds; and some die from wounds after fighting each other over territory.

Being so regular in their habits over such long periods, badgers are also betrayed by well-defined runs – paths that they have made and maintained over the years by constant use, leading to foraging areas, watering places, play areas, sunbathing sites and other setts. They will persist in using these routes even when obstructions are put in their way, and all too often this leads to their deaths. Wiser construction engineers and builders make allowances for the badgers, creating tunnels under roads or hanging badger gates in new fences so that the badgers can continue to use their ancient highways. They may range over considerable distances in their search for food.

Grubbing about

Badgers are omnivores – they will eat almost anything, be it animal or vegetable – and are great opportunists. They tend to be more carnivorous in spring and summer, when snacks include the young of various small mammals such as rabbits, rodents and moles, and also frogs. They eat earthworms above all (an adult badger can eat a hundred or two on a warm wet night), slugs, snails, beetles, wasp grubs, leatherjackets, cockchafer grubs and large caterpillars. They eat dead things – fresh carrion in winter (but not rotting), which might include stillborn lambs as well as dead birds. They love fruit and nuts of all kinds, root vegetables, grains and maize; they also eat fungi, bluebell bulbs and a fair amount of clover, grass and other greenstuffs.

BEING BADGERED?

As well as providing endless hours of interesting viewing, badgers are on your side by helping to reduce populations of various grubs and caterpillars, young rabbits, field voles and woodmice, and digging out wasp nests. On the other hand, they sometimes make your lawn look like a battlefield as they tear into the grass searching for those grubs at certain times of year, especially in late autumn, sometimes even rolling back the turf as they forage. They will probably steal your raspberries and potatoes, carrots and sweetcorn; they'll vacuum up windfall apples and possibly break low branches as they climb into the tree for fruit. They might tip over your rubbish bin for a good scavenge, but then again it might have already been tipped over by some other culprit. They dig holes in fields; they might trample on grain crops; they scratch elder trees and occasionally bite at the bark low down on sycamore trees to get at the sweet sap.

Very rarely does a badger do enough damage to a garden to be considered economically a pest, except by breaking down fences. It's more an offence to the lawn owner's aesthetic senses, or an annoyance to the vegetable grower when the sweetcorn that would have been ready for the table in a day or two disappears overnight. Most badger incursions are seasonal, so if you have enough patience, the 'nuisance' will soon be over for another year.

Gentle persuasion

If you really cannot live with your local badgers, think very carefully before acting and remember that the law is heavily on the side of the badger. The only legal deterrents you can use are certain chemicals classified specifically for use in deterring badgers, and then only in certain circumstances, or erecting physical barriers to prevent access to your land (but not to keep badgers away from their sett). Seek advice from a local badger protection group or from the RSPCA.

The main points to remember when trying to discourage badgers from 'annoying' you are that they are powerful animals and extremely dangerous if cornered (for example, inadvertently in a shed), and that badgers are creatures of

habit and have a strong urge to continue to do whatever
their forebears have always done, wherever they have
always done it. If you try to fence off their customary route,
they simply barge through, dig underneath or climb over.
Badgers are very determined animals and you are unlikely
to win the fencing war. The fence needs to be scratch- and
bite-proof, of strong mesh at least 125cm (4ft) high, dug at
least 50cm (20in) into the ground and with a 50cm (20in)
turnout to prevent digging, with a protective concrete sill
under any gateways.

You really do need to respect their prior claims and if
your garden is simply somewhere they pass through on
their way to somewhere else, you should let them continue
to do so by installing a two-way badger gate in the fence at
exactly the point where they have always crossed that
boundary. Badger gates swing from the top and are too
heavy for animals other than badgers to push through: they
are usually made of wiremesh set in a heavy frame
measuring about 30 × 18cm (12 × 7in). Some people try to
divert badgers from their regular paths by laying trails of
peanuts and syrup along a different route, but the route
must lead eventually to where the badgers were going
anyway. An alternative is to install a low-voltage, two-
strand electric fence, with one strand at about 7.5cm (3in)
from the ground and the other at 20cm (8in) high, with a line
of polytape at the base. You could perhaps use electric sheep
netting but don't use electric rabbit flexinetting: it might
entangle a hedgehog.

Desperate gardeners have tried various remedies,
including things that flap in the wind or flashing traffic
lamps, or filling the garden at night with floodlight – which
is pointless as badgers quickly get used to the lights and get
on with doing whatever it was they came to do. In any case,
you are polluting the night sky and keeping your

neighbours awake! More practical ideas are to use bungees to secure your dustbin lids if bin raiding is a problem, and to make your garden less attractive in the first place by ensuring there is no interesting badger food around: don't put tempting scraps on an open compost heap, for example, and don't leave birdfood out overnight. Some have tried the extreme remedy of using insecticides and other means of removing badger favourites such as worms from the garden, but that's just plain crazy (think through the ramifications).

Most of the smelly deterrents simply don't work, even if they are legal. The products approved for badgers are not smellies but taste repellents designed to protect crops. The problem is that they taste nasty to humans as well, and you must refrain from using them on any food crops for several weeks before harvest. It just might be worth trying them on the lawn.

It might seem perverse, but in a hot dry spell in summer or in a cold hard winter, when badgers find it difficult to dig for food, you could try feeding them deliberately in a part of the garden where they feel safe and you don't feel offended by them.

'SLINKIES'

The rest of the mustelid family are much slinkier than the badger and most are unlikely to be considered as 'pests' except by the occasional gamekeeper or perhaps poultry owners. Most of them in fact do you a favour by hunting a wide range of other 'pests', especially rodents and rabbits. The 'slinkies' include weasels, stoats, polecats (and ferrets), pine martens, mink and otters. All of these animals have long slender bodies, short legs and small rounded ears. They are all pure carnivores – they eat meat (including fish in some cases). Highly athletic and efficient hunters with a characteristic bounding motion on land, they kill cleanly, with a quick bite to the back of the victim's neck. You will, however, be lucky to see any of these supreme hunters, even in areas where they are quite common.

The challenge for poultry keepers is that no such dedicated carnivore can resist the fluster of feathers in a confined space and most will kill far more than they need for immediate consumption. The most likely culprits are stoats, polecats and mink. A carnivore's life can be a difficult one and it's a matter of seizing the opportunity that has been presented to them on a plate. It is better to ensure that the carnivore cannot enter the confined space of a chicken run in the first place than to slaughter every 'slinky' you see.

Mink and otters

Mink are aliens: in the wild they all originated from escaped or deliberately released animals that are native to North America and were first imported into Britain by fur farmers in the late 1920s. They have been breeding in the wild here for half a century and have spread to many parts of the country, wherever there are rivers or lakes and marshes.

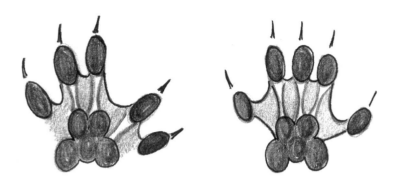

Mink's footprints

They are good swimmers, with partially webbed feet, and hunt for fish (putting themselves in direct competition with otters and anglers), waterfowl, rabbits, voles and rats, with an occasional raid on poultry or gamebirds and, anecdotally, homing pigeons, puppies and kittens.

In the wild, mink reach up to 66cm (2ft 2in) in length from nose to tail tip and weigh up to 1.8kg (4lb). The coat is very dark brown all through, but the offspring of more recent escapees might vary in colour. The tail is bushier than those of the small mustelids.

Mink can be very bad news for the wellbeing of local wildlife and poultry, but don't mistake otters for them. Otters are larger and have a tapering tail, with a very thick base, and a flattened head with prominent whiskers sprouting from the muzzle. You can also tell an otter from a mink by its swimming style: the mink swims more jerkily while the otter swims smoothly, producing a big V-shaped wake. When an otter comes out of the water its brown, glossy coat remains spiky; its throat is paler whereas most mink are uniformly dark chocolate brown.

Otters are gradually making a comeback, carefully helped by human hands in some places. They are superb swimmers and depend on fish, crustaceans and aquatic insects; thus they always live in lakes, rivers, streams or marshes. Occasionally they will take birds, small mammals and amphibians but these are not a major part of their diet. On land they look cumbersome but can move as fast as a human can over short distances. They are usually nocturnal and very shy of humans after many years of persecution.

Pine martens

These handsome mustelids are less slinky than their smaller relations and have longer legs, bigger ears, hairy feet and a big bushy tail. The coat is rich chocolate with an obvious cream to light orange throat patch. They are now a protected species, mainly confined to coniferous woodland in the Scottish Highlands, parts of Wales, the Lake District and Ireland. Active by day, they are great climbers with an almost squirrel-like style and agility, but are just as likely to hunt on the ground. Their prey is mainly rodents (especially field voles) and small birds such as tits and wrens, but they also eat a range of seasonal food, including eggs, carrion, fish, beetles, caterpillars, frogs, bumble bees, rabbits, moths and berries.

Polecats and ferrets

Polecats have a characteristic mask: a broad dark band right across the face, including the eyes, with white areas above and below. The rest of the coat looks generally dark but with a creamy undercoat to soften and diffuse the colour. Polecats hunt mainly by night and have become rare in Britain except for their stronghold in Wales, from which they are gradually spreading again. They are expert and ruthless hunters and go for whatever they can find – rabbits, hares, mice, voles, hedgehogs, birds, eggs, frogs, lizards, insect larvae and worms.

Ferrets are domesticated animals and likely to be much less fearful of people. Most of the ferrets you stumble across have got lost after a rabbiting expedition with their owners or have escaped simply because ferrets enjoy the challenge of escaping through impossibly small holes and gaps. They will probably be only too glad to be recaptured and you can either pick them up (as long as you know how to handle a ferret properly) or lure them into a pipe – they can't resist investigating it. Take care: a worried ferret might well bite and, when it bites, it hangs on; painful, but not life-threatening to a human being.

Weasels and stoats

Weasels are so small that it is hard to credit them with being killers. You usually just see a quick streak of chestnut and white, or you might see a weasel standing bolt upright, for all the world like a meerkat glancing about to see what's what. They are the smallest of the mustelids, weighing anything from 35 to 200g (1¼ to 7oz) and measuring from 17 to 23cm (6½ to 9in), excluding the relatively short tail.

Weasels are active by day as well as by night. Their main prey befits their size: voles and mice, whose burrows weasels are small enough to enter. They are also small enough to sneak into bird nesting boxes. They will eat worms but are brave enough to tackle rats and even rabbits and squirrels, especially when they gang up. A weasel needs to eat the equivalent of 25 to 30 per cent of its own

Trail of a running weasel

Trail of a bounding stoat

bodyweight daily, which means at least one vole or mouse a day. In theory, a local family of weasels could work their way through about 2,000 rodents a year.

Weasels sometimes enter houses, quite by mistake, and are only too glad to be shown the way out. A case could be made for taming a weasel and encouraging it to deal with house rodents if they are a problem. You'd have to start with a youngster.

You are more likely to see a stoat than a weasel, because weasels spend so much of their time hunting down holes and because stoats seem quite fearless of you. Stoats, too, are active by day as well as by night and the species look so alike that it is easy to mistake one for the other. In general, most stoats are larger than most weasels but the main identifying feature is that stoats have a black tip to their much longer tail. In some parts of Britain stoats grow a white coat in winter, but the black tail tip remains – and this is what, in the House of Lords, you would recognise as ermine. In summer all stoats are russet to sandy-coloured above and creamy underneath, with a clear demarcation between the two; weasels don't have such an obvious straight line separating the colours.

The main prey for stoats are rabbits, which may weigh three or four times as much as the hunter does. A stoat will pursue a particular rabbit victim so relentlessly that quite often the latter simply submits to its inevitable fate and stands rooted to the spot, squealing horribly, without even trying to outrun its nemesis and in some cases dying of fright before the stoat has so much as laid a tooth on it. Stoats also go for rats, mice, voles and birds, including, it has to be admitted, gamebirds and sometimes poultry, and they do tend to kill to excess in a confined situation.

Weasel's footprints

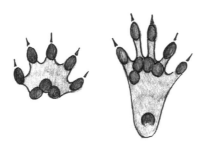

Stoat's footprints

Bats, Bless 'Em

What is it about bats? Some people are crazy about them; most are wary and quite a few seem to be utterly terrified of these tiny, harmless creatures that do no damage at all to your person or your property and only ask to be left in peace. Once you have plucked up courage (if that's what it takes) to look at a bat more closely, you will be amazed at how small and fragile it is and how appealing it can be. Its actual body, under all that meticulously groomed thick fur, might be thinner than a fat felt-tip marker pen – about 1cm (½in) – in the little pipistrelle, a type of small brownish bat. It is the only mammal that is a true flier rather than simply an opportunistic glider and it can remain on the wing for hours.

There is no reason at all to be afraid of bats, but bats have every reason to be afraid of you, even though they are now very heavily protected by the law. It is illegal to disturb bats at roost, for example, let alone to injure or kill them. It is also illegal to damage a roost site or obstruct the bat's entry to it. If work needs to be done on a roof or in a roof-space where bats are known to roost, you must time the work to ensure that there is as little disruption to the bats as possible.

Many years ago, as a small child, I lived for a time in the wilds of Wiltshire in a magically ancient house with tall mullioned windows and stone flag floors. It had a secret tunnel to the abbey; it had ghosts; it had mice rampaging behind the wainscotting; it had fairies all over the garden (in my childish imagination, at least); and it had bats that would fly in through open windows on summer evenings and just as merrily fly out again after doing a quick circuit of the high-ceilinged rooms in search of moths. As a child I was quite happy to have the bats swooping around – it was the moths batting against the light bulbs that unsettled me with their agitated flapping – but I clearly remember a large retired admiral, much decorated during the war, chasing the bats with a tennis racquet while his equally large old labrador cowered under the bed, presumably more alarmed by the admiral's antics than by the bats.

During the nineteenth century and the earlier years of the twentieth, people were always trying to devise ways of ridding their homes of bats, by methods that ranged from ingenious dissuasion to violence. All of these would now be illegal and I have no intention of describing those methods here (the milder ones involved stuffed owls and constant lighting). My aim is to encourage you to learn to live with your bats and come to like them.

In Britain, there are fifteen resident species of bat – most of them in the southern counties – and none of them have the remotest tendency towards vampirism. About half a dozen are widespread; all the rest are either becoming or are already rare, some almost to the point of extinction.

Bats are actually a blessing. Their diet is entirely based on insects, especially moths, flying beetles, assorted flies and all those little midgy things that teem in gardens anywhere near water and woodland and spoil your summer evening barbecue. Hence bats do their hunting wherever the insects are to be found, especially along the edges of woods or tall hedgerows, along riverbanks, over ponds and other damp places, or in the confines of sheltered gardens and churchyards. Most of them catch their food on the wing – sometimes literally, by scooping up a large insect with their wing. Some have perfected the art of hovering over shrubbery to grab their prey; some can be seen skimming at speed over the water and catching prey in their mouths or simply snatching a quick sip of water to quench their thirst. Some eat while flying; others perch somewhere for their meal.

DES. RES.

Bats need somewhere to roost – a place to rest during the day (they hunt mainly between sunset and sunrise), a place to preserve precious energy in winter, and a place to mate, to give birth and to rear their young. With so many of their old roosting environments such as decaying trees, big old barns and caves or tunnels disappearing or access to them being denied in one way or another, bats increasingly take refuge in the loftspace of houses, including nice new ones that offer much better accommodation than some of the older buildings. Like many other species of wildlife, bats are creatures of habit and, once they have found a desirable residence, they tend to return to it year after year.

That ideal home remains at a fairly even temperature when bats become torpid during their winter hibernation, with no extremes of heat or cold and preferably no draughts. Direct sunlight is generally avoided, but the well-inhabited south-facing roof space in my cottage becomes as hot as Hades in summer and the bats persist in using it. The atmosphere of the roost needs to be more humid than dry; and the site must not be disturbed by noisy or nosy humans or by predators (mainly cats, or occasionally opportunistic owls). There needs to be a convenient, very small access hole or slit of some kind. Bats are so tiny that they can squeeze into all sorts of unlikely places; for example, you might find them sound asleep in the spaces of a cavity wall (make quite sure there are no bats in residence before you have such walls pumped full of insulation foam), or tucked under a tile, roof-felt or lead flashing. A bat is quite capable of creeping under a draughty door or through a gap left by a careless plumber when a pipe is installed, and this is why you might sometimes find a surprised bat inside the room. It doesn't actually want to be in there at all – it just got lost and wants you to leave the window open so that it can escape during the night.

Bats quite often change roosts, or use different roosts for different purposes. In my own cottage, I have a mixture of long-eared, whiskered and serotine bats and some of them use it in winter to hibernate while others prefer it as a nursery roost. It is intriguing to watch the different species emerging at different times in the evening – always in the same order. There are not many bats in my loft; in fact, I feel quite ashamed when I do a June bat count and struggle to reach thirty, whereas in another cottage I lived with literally hundreds of pipistrelles – far too many to count but it was a joy to watch them pouring out in the evening to chase insects on the ponds and streams. The pipistrelles would chatter away to each other (a sound that is much too gentle and entertaining to be intrusive) as if having a neighbourly discussion about the evening's prospects before launching themselves into the dusk. There was a drawback: I was asked to set up an overnight moth-trap using a mercury lamp. In the morning I eagerly investigated the night's catch, preparing to release my moths into an old barn to hide up during the day. Sadly, I found a lot of moths' wings and very few whole moths: the pipistrelles had had a fantastic midnight feast on all the hundreds of amazing moths (some of them huge and dramatically coloured) that had been attracted to the lamp!

Very rarely did any of the pipistrelles enter the house and then it was usually a youngster by mistake. I'd find it in the morning hidden in the folds of a curtain, perhaps, and gently carry it out to rest in the barn for the day until it could join the mob in the evening. The tiny, fragile creature would immediately hang itself upside down on the barn timbers, or even on my fingers as I carried it. Sometimes you might find a stranded bat on the ground outside the roost in daylight and again this is usually a youngster, which needs rescuing from any local cats. In theory you should not handle a bat yourself unless you are licensed to do so, but if it is in danger, you should move it to a place of safety, preferably as close to the roost as possible or perhaps in the protective ivy of a nearby tree. In all other circumstances, summon help from your local bat group. Bats need all the help they can get.

BATS IN THE BELFRY

The old phrase 'bats in the belfry' is misleading. Firstly, bats are most unlikely to hang out in a belfry: they'd be a nervous wreck at the first hint of a bell's clapper heading for the metal. Secondly, bats are not mad. There are many other myths about bats and being blind is one of them. They are colourblind but they can see quite well and probably better than you can in twilight. But far more important to them than sight is their acute sense of hearing, which is especially sensitive to very high-frequency sounds, and, as everyone knows, they hunt not by sight but by their amazing inbuilt radar or echo-location system.

Another myth about bats is the old wives' tale that they will get themselves tangled up in your hair. Bats have no desire to nest in your hair. They might swoop rather close if there are small insects hovering just above you (which is often the case) but with a radar system that has pinpoint accuracy on a midge, it is hardly likely that a bat is going to collide with something as big as your head.

There are other misconceptions. I was having some building work done by an elderly builder, a good country boy who took much pleasure in birdwatching. 'I've always wondered,' he said, 'why it is I've never found a bat's nest in a roof, and anyway how do they manage to lay their eggs upside down?' He was joking, of course, and was well aware that bats, being mammals, give birth to live young; eggs and nests have nothing to do with it.

Bats mate in the autumn and winter but fertilisation is delayed until spring. Because the rate of development of the embryo (British bats usually have only one baby at a time) depends on the availability of food for the mother and on warmth, the mother usually seeks out a nursery roost that is relatively warm. This tends to be with a group of other mums-to-be; the father (a promiscuous type) is not welcome in the nursery roost. The young are born in about June or July, after an average gestation period of perhaps 50 days – depending to a large extent on the weather, as development can grind to a temporary halt if the weather is bad. For the birth, the mother usually hangs head upwards rather than upside down, which sounds like a very dangerous way to be born, suspended over a void, but there are rarely any catastrophes and the baby begins to suckle almost immediately.

Baby bats are suckled for several weeks. They grow quickly and when three weeks old they might start to try out their wings now and then. The wings are leathery membranes stretched in between the very long 'fingers' and also between the fifth finger and the ankle. In some species wings are also handy as cloaks in which the bat can wrap itself to preserve body heat.

BAT HABITS

Bats generally stay in the roost during the day but don't be surprised to find them out and about in daylight occasionally, especially in winter, when they might take advantage of a mild spell to stretch their wings and see if there is any food about. Wintering bats become torpid but they don't just zonk out for several months: they move about in the roost, get themselves a drink, and might even shift to another roost if the conditions at home aren't quite right. For most of them, the roost temperature needs to be between 0 and 10°C (32 and 50°F), depending on the species, and their body temperature drops to more or less the same as their surroundings. The same is true in summer during the day: their body temperature is the same as the ambient temperature in the roost, which means anything from a cool 15°C (59°F), say, to a roasting 40°C (104°F) under a hot roof – though at such an extreme they will probably take steps to cool down.

As the time for emergence approaches in the evening, there is plenty of moving about, chattering and gossiping, and jockeying for position. Like bumble bees, bats shiver to warm up to flying temperature if the roost is cool. Usually the time of exit is as regular as clockwork and again varies according to species: my long-eared bats always leave it very late, until the light has faded so much I can hardly believe my eyes, but species such as noctules are much less shy and emerge soon after sunset. It depends on the lifestyle of the prey: different species of bat eat different species of insect and, naturally, they go hunting when those insects are most likely to be active.

My long-eareds tend to set off in exactly the same direction every time, before dispersing to favoured hunting grounds; they seem to be out for an hour or two and maybe return to the roost (usually to catch the moths that are attracted by lights at upstairs windows) and then come out for another fly-around shortly before dawn. If the weather is poor on a particular day and the insects are unlikely to be plentiful, bats will often not emerge at all that evening even in summer. Insects are less likely to be abroad in wet or windy weather, or when the temperature is less than about 10°C (50°F), and apparently they are also less likely to be flying in bright moonlight. So, for a bat, the ideal dinner weather is calm, warm and cloudy.

Friend or foe?

Quite apart from psychological aversions to bats, people sometimes think that bats might cause some sort of damage in their loft. Bats are not rodents: they don't chew anything except insects, they are incapable of gnawing and they don't make beds or nests. The roost is simply somewhere to hang out, literally: they will attach themselves to a beam or rafter, for example, by their toenails and don't damage anything at all. While they are in your roof, they will probably eat up the adults of any harmful beetles – deathwatch and other flying insects whose grubs can destroy house timbers. Incidentally, take very great care with any chemicals used for treating woodworm: these can kill bats as well as beetles and larvae, and persist in the timbers for years. Ask for bat-friendly woodworm treatment.

In the garden the bats will gobble up the mosquitoes for you and it has been claimed that a roost of a hundred pipistrelles will devour at least one and half million gnats in just one month – and possibly as many as nine million.

Some people think bat droppings are a problem. There certainly will be droppings under the roost but they are surprisingly 'clean' ones and very easy to sweep up at intervals if you are worried about them. They make a good extra layer of roof insulation and could also be used as fertiliser. Unlike rodent droppings, they are dry and crumbly and they don't harbour disease, and unlike the droppings of carnivores, they don't stink, though you might detect a slight 'batty' odour if you let them accumulate too much or if conditions are not fairly dry. Bats much prefer clean quarters anyway and are pretty fussy about personal hygiene. If droppings are causing you problems, real or imaginary, spread out some plastic sheeting under the roosting area indoors (mainly under a ridge beam or near the exit hole) and remove them from time to time. Outside the exit hole, you could fix some kind of ledge to catch the droppings as they fall before they reach ground level. Come winter, you'll hardly find any droppings anyway.

All in all, and quite apart from the legislation that protects them, you would do far better to learn to live with and love your bats than to make them feel unwelcome. As ever, the fear or distaste soon goes once you learn more about them and study their ways. They are beautiful and sensitive little creatures and they thoroughly deserve your interest and protection.

Gnawers and Nibblers

It is among the rodents that the major household pests are found. However delightful they might be as individuals, in general rodents are gnawers (which can mean damage) and some of them tend to eat what humans like to eat (which means they are in direct competition with us). Some of them carry diseases that can make people exceedingly ill. So, although you might be happy to accommodate some of the rodents – and indeed several species are in need of protection rather than persecution – with others you really do have to act to prevent potential problems such as food contamination and electric wires being chewed through.

WHAT WAS THAT?

The first step, as ever, is to know your species. Rodents are characterised by their chisel-edged front teeth, or incisors, which grow continuously – hence that constant gnawing.

The group includes beavers (once native to Britain but no longer), coypu (a fur-bearing South American escapee that became a pest in East Anglia in the 1950s and has since been rigorously controlled), squirrels, dormice, rats, mice and voles.

Shrews, with those characteristic very long pointed snouts, are not rodents. They are carnivorous or insectivorous and are nonstop eaters with a very high metabolic rate, constantly on the go and doing a great job in breaking down animal matter and recycling it into the soil. Their only potential for being a nuisance to human beings is that their corpses tend to be left lying around by cats, which will hunt them but rarely actually eat them. The group includes the common shrew (see the trail above, complete with tail print), pygmy shrew, greater and lesser white-toothed shrews, and the dear little water shrew that you sometimes glimpse as not much more than a trail of silver bubbles in a clean stream or watercress beds.

Dormice

The native common dormouse is small, harmless and enchanting and is becoming increasingly rare because of the loss of its habitat in England and Wales; the southeast corner of England is where it is most likely to be found today. It is nocturnal and spends about six months of the year in hibernation. It is instantly set apart from other mice by its furry tail and is a much smaller animal than its even bushier-tailed cousin, the fat or edible dormouse, which was introduced into Hertfordshire at the beginning of the twentieth century. The edible dormouse, a native of southern and eastern Europe, has not spread far from Tring, but if you happen to live in that area, you might find an edible dormouse snuffling and scampering about in your loft during the night and possibly raiding your fruit. Apple lofts are an edible dormouse's idea of paradise. You might mistake it for a rather small squirrel.

Voles

You can tell a vole from a mouse quite easily. Overall, it is sort of rounder. Its coat is longer and shaggier; its nose is blunt rather than pointy; its eyes and ears are small; and its tail is comparatively short. Voles don't do much harm usually, other than startling you as they rush about their business in the garden, shooting across the grass from one area of cover to another. Field voles sometimes create minor havoc in pasture but they won't be a problem on a mown lawn. Voles are unlikely to use your house, unless the cat brings one in and releases it.

Bank voles

Bank voles are also eaten by many birds of prey and carnivores. These small, deep-chestnut animals are diligent burrowers, making tunnels with a nest in the middle lined with grass, leaves, moss and feathers, a few centimetres below ground, or nesting a little way up a tree trunk, perhaps hidden in ivy. Don't be surprised if you find their tunnels under a piece of corrugated iron or corrugated plastic that has been lying on the ground for a while.

They are more likely to be near woodland or hedges with plenty of thick cover, rather than out in the middle of a field. You might see them, scuttling at speed, during the day or during the night. If you see a vole climbing, it's a bank vole, not a field vole (I often see bank voles scrambling about in an ageing hedge of flowering currant mixed with wild brambles). Their tastes are catholic: they eat fleshy fruits (they love the flesh of rosehips), hazel nuts and soft seeds;

they also eat fungi, leaves, grass, roots, moss, flowers and maybe a little taste of elder or larch after stripping the bark, and they occasionally take insects, including moth cocoons, and worms.

Field voles

Some of the voles are under threat. Even the field vole, which is the main dish on the menu for a very wide range of predators, is losing its habitat because of changes in farming practice. When vole numbers drop, so do those of their predators – such as stoats, weasels, barn owls, little owls,

Voles and mice are easy to distinguish: the field vole shows the typically blunt-nosed vole profile, with smaller eyes and ears than a mouse, and has a shorter tail

Field vole's footprints

tawny owls and assorted day-flying birds of prey. Field voles live mainly on grass leaves and stems and most of them prefer to live in rough grassland, where they create regular runways through the forest of matted grasses, hidden from view – they are active by day and by night and good cover is vital. You can often hear the chattering and rustling of field voles before you see them.

Water voles

The lovable water vole ('Ratty' in *Wind in the Willows*) is in serious trouble, partly because of loss of habitat and partly because of predation by mink. I have been lucky enough to live near ponds and streams for many years and still get a thrill whenever I see a chubby-faced water vole, though

Water voles are not rats: they have tiny ears and, unlike rats,
often seem unaware of danger

such occasions are now rare. They have this delightful habit of sitting on a little mudflat island in the stream, hunched over with rounded shoulders and systematically chomping their way down a stem of grass or rushes clutched between the paws like a length of Brighton rock. They are rather messy eaters, leaving plenty of food debris at their regular feeding stations.

Sometimes called water rats, water voles should never be confused with the common rat. Water voles are about the same size as a rat, which adds to the confusion, but they have a proportionately shorter tail, very small ears that you can hardly see in the fur and a short, more rounded face. The coat is shaggier and browner than a rat's; it doesn't have that grey tinge to it. The droppings are different too: a water vole's are smooth and cylindrical, with rounded rather than tapered ends, and their colour reflects the leafy diet – they are pale green to khaki.

Water voles always live near water and are expert swimmers (but don't be fooled, as the common rat is also a good swimmer) and good divers when danger threatens. On dry land, water voles are rather clumsy, whereas a rat is nimble. Also, water voles are more likely to be active during the day, while rats are mainly nocturnal. One thing is for sure: water voles won't invade your house, so if it's scampering you hear in your loft, it's a rat.

Water vole's footprints

DRAT! IT'S A RAT!

Rats make the most delightful pets. They have very clean habits, they are playful and affectionate (yes, they do recognise you as an individual) and they are highly intelligent. Unfortunately, their wild relatives have a deservedly bad reputation for spreading disease, harking back to the terrible days of the plague. They still harbour other very unpleasant diseases that can be passed to humans, such as leptospiroris. They take or contaminate your food, chew your pipes and wires, gnaw on your woodwork and generally make very bad neighbours. It is probably fair to say that the majority of people have an almost instinctive dislike of rats and shudder at the sight of them. The fear will vanish if you take the trouble to understand them and know their little ways, but for reasons of hygiene you still need to dissuade them from hanging around your home.

There are two species of rat in Britain. The black ship's rat is typically an urban animal but is now very localised in Britain and you are only likely to come across them in major seaports, where they find a living in dockland warehouses. The common rat, on the other hand, is ubiquitous. Urban, rural, wherever – it's not that choosy, as long as there is an

Brown rat

ample supply of food. Farmyards are good news for rats, so are warehouses, grain stores, rubbish tips and sewers (don't ask). And so are cities and towns, with all those lovely take-away discards, uncollected binbags and other food available wherever a rat looks.

Most people have no difficulty in recognising a rat on sight, with its long, scaly tail and pointed muzzle and above all by its size, which definitely means it isn't just a mouse. Rats tend to scurry at a quick trot when they know where they are going, but at other times they wander at a more leisurely pace, with the rolling gait of a sailor. If something is chasing them, they can cover the ground at speed in a series of bounding leaps and can also swim and dive to safety.

Rats are basically nocturnal and you are most likely to see them around dusk, and again from about 3 a.m. until dawn, though you might see them around in daylight if they feel safe. They tend to live in family colonies and are very sociable with each other. They won't tolerate intruders and you'll hear plenty of squealing if there's a squabble going on. Some of the sounds made by rats are too high for humans to hear. Rats have a very acute sense of hearing, and of smell, but relatively poor eyesight. If you catch a rat by torchlight, you will see the dull red glow of its eyes reflecting the beam.

Actually, a rat would rather not be seen and is much more scared of you than you are of it. Being scared, they are pretty dangerous when cornered: they attack in self-defence but are most unlikely to attack without provocation. They are not predators out to harm humans. Also, rats are creatures of habit and deeply suspicious of something new in their environment, which you need to remember if you are taking steps to trap or poison them.

Rats eat almost anything edible and some things that you wouldn't have thought were edible, such as soap and candles. Their preference is for food that is rich in proteins and starch, and cereals are ideal. They also relish fruit, meat, cheese, fish, bones and urban scraps. In the countryside, apart from raiding cereal crops, they will eat anything from weed seeds to crabs and earthworms and will make inroads on root crops and brassicas.

A well-fed rat can produce up to five litters of young a year, with an average of seven or eight babies in each litter. Young female rats are mature by only eleven weeks old. Breeding is continuous throughout the year if food supplies remain good.

Apart from actually seeing a rat, you can look for other evidence of their presence. You can also smell them, especially the urine. Their droppings are bigger than a mouse's and usually more than 1cm (½in) long, often tapering at one end or both and often deposited in groups. Rat burrows are characteristic: the earth dug out of the burrow remains in a heap near the entrance, which is perhaps 6 to 9cm (2½ to 3½in) in diameter. They prefer to make their burrows in a bank or slope for good drainage, or underneath something – perhaps paving or other flat stones, or protected by tree roots or a pile of logs. You might find evidence of regular rat runs, about 5 to 10cm (2 to 4in) wide; these might be obvious as trampled earth paths but they might also be no more than a shallow depression in the grass. Indoors, look for dark, greasy smears where the rats regularly brush against walls and timbers.

While the rats might be using your house as a run or as a larder, fortunately they are more likely to make their nests somewhere else. Common rats prefer to nest on or near the ground, though ship's rats will make themselves at home in buildings and nest quite high up, maybe in the roof space.

The first step in any war with rats is to remove whatever it is that attracts them, especially food. In the garden, be very careful about birdfood and never leave any around overnight. Don't put tasty titbits on an open compost heap: if you want to recycle kitchen waste, use an enclosed wormery bin but remember that rats and other rodents can squeeze through surprisingly small holes to reach goodies. Use a ratproof metal dustbin for your rubbish. If you keep poultry, any rats in the area will soon discover the joys of chickenfeed and their very presence will unsettle the birds so much that they'll stop laying. And it's no good telling the chickens that the rats are after the grain, not after the birds themselves.

Germaine Greer wrote a trenchant newspaper article about the rats that were rampant on her smallholding, with tales of rats 'dragging sleeping doves off their perches' as well as entering her home to eat the dogs' food, defecate and urinate in the kitchen cupboards and gnaw through the bedroom floor 'so that they can feast on my toenails'. Even so, she abhorred poisoning as she had seen rats going through their dying throes. And even she admitted that the rats had as much right to her house as she did – it was simply that she didn't choose to share it with them.

At least she didn't try some of the more unpleasant remedies suggested in the eighteenth and nineteenth centuries. J Baxter of Lewes, for example, suggested cutting a sponge into small pieces which were then fried and dipped in honey. They were placed in pans of shallow water near wherever the rats were living. The rats would eat the sponges and then wash them down with the water. The sponges would swell and . . . Another trick was to slice corks into thin discs and roast them in grease; the unsuspecting rat that devoured them would die of indigestion. But even Baxter deplored the use of poison – not for the sake of the rat, but because it would die indoors and stink the place out, and because, in his time, 'scarcely does a week pass without an inquest being held upon the body of some unfortunate being, who, by the negligence of individuals employing this poison, has met with an untimely death'. Instead, he suggested a recipe that included opium, sugar, flour and a few other ingredients that you are unlikely to be able to purchase across the counter today. Apparently, powdered ratsbane would kill 'any animal born blind' without pain, very suddenly, in the act of eating the stuff. In farmyards the remedy was the simple old one of putting stacks and grain stores out of reach on stone pillars (the old stone-mushroom trick) but with the added touch of encasing the pillars in slippery tin.

Because rats carry disease, owners of commercial, industrial or agricultural premises who know that they have rodents are legally obliged to take steps to eradicate them. If you suspect that you have a rat problem at home, your first source of help will be your local council's environmental health department, who will send out their vermin control officer.

The main methods of rat control are trapping or poisoning and none of them is ideal. With traps, for example, the kill is not always clean, which is horrific for any animal, and also rats tend to be 'trap-shy' because of their suspiciousness of anything new. As for poison, many rats are resistant – either because they have become 'super-rats' that are not killed by the poison, or because they don't eat it anyway, as long as they have another source of food. Some of the poisons are not at all kind in the way in which they kill, and there is always the concern about other animals finding either the poison or the poisoned carcase, though most of the modern poisons are rat-specific. Search through some of the organic gardening catalogues for other ideas but be wary of sonic devices: some of the reports in scientific journals are less than enthusiastic about their success rates. It seems that they are more effective if their position is changed frequently.

There is talk of biological control. Back in the 1970s, when I was touring council refuse dumps in the interests of research into recycling, I was told that they had been trying out a contraceptive pill for rats to reduce the population at the dump. Another idea was to release sterile rats into the general rat community so that, gradually, the population would reduce by lack of propagation. Or, by genetic modification, the scientists could create rats with a gene that would be lethal when expressed in the offspring – sci fi with a vengeance, and a pretty sneaky way to treat any fellow creature. Then there was the suggestion of sedation – slipping something into the rats' food that would lull them to sleep . . . and then what? You would then be faced with the same problem as with kindly live trapping.

You could get a resident terrier or cat and let them deal with your rats. It's a much 'greener' method than poisoning or GM: death is instantaneous and the very presence of such a predator is probably enough to make any sensible rat think hard about staying around. You could also encourage wild predators such as foxes, which will catch adult rats; most other predators, including owls and stoats, usually find an adult rat too much of a fighter but they will certainly help themselves to young ones.

Whatever you do, don't let rats take over, as once they become established in your garden, your sheds or your house, it will be a major operation to clear the existing population and you will have to be on constant guard against a new mob moving into what is obviously a desirable area.

MICE

Foxes, cats and terriers will also control mice, of course. Mice might be a bit of a nuisance in the garden or in the house but you don't necessarily have to kill the little dears. Again, mice can make delightful pets when they are bred for the purpose and very often give children their first chance to care for a living animal.

Garden mice

In the garden, mice are in their element. They might steal the seeds you have just sown, or help themselves to birdfood, or raid stored apples, or chew bark at the base of a sapling, or nibble at your crocus flowers or daffodil bulbs, or nip off your seedlings, or make shredded-paper nests in the garden shed, or . . . well, you get the picture. To know how to deal with outdoor problems, you need to get to know your mouse.

There are three species that might be so cheeky. Two are true country mice: the wood mouse and the closely related but larger yellow-necked mouse. The third is the house mouse, which can be naughty in the garden as well as in the house. All three can be told apart from voles by their sharper faces, big eyes and ears, and longer tails.

The wood mouse is also known as the long-tailed field mouse. It's a pretty little thing, with bigger rather bulging eyes and bigger ears than a house mouse, and a coat that is dark brown to sandy with a yellowish look on the flanks and with pale grey underside (a house mouse is more of a dreary greyish brown on top and not much lighter underneath). Its long tail is very lightly furred, in contrast to the more obviously scaly and thicker tail of a house mouse, and it

Trail of a wood mouse

Wood mouse, richer in colour than a house mouse and with larger feet and a proportionately longer tail.

doesn't have that house-mousy smell. The yellow-necked mouse is broadly similar to the wood mouse but larger, heavier, more butch, bolder and more aggressive, with a richer coat colour and a distinctive broad yellow collar round its neck and down its chest like a big broad cross.

The yellow-neck is more likely to object to being handled and will probably squeak angrily and give you a bit of a nip, though I do know of people who have tamed their yellow-necks. Wood mice are equally likely to squeal if caught. Both species have many, many enemies: they are preyed upon by buzzards, owls, falcons, hawks, corvids, herons, foxes, stoats and weasels (and even moles, apparently), and of course by cats. In my own garden I've seen pheasants and chickens occasionally catching, playing with and swallowing young wood mice.

Wood mice are more ground-based than yellow-necks, which are excellent climbers and quite happy scampering into trees and along the branches a very long way up. Yellow-necks find climbing into a loft is a doddle and frequently do so. Both establish regular routes and I often

Trail of a yellow-necked mouse

*Yellow-necked mouse –
its characteristic yellow
collar contrasts with its
very pale underside*

see them making a dash for it across the garden path where
the gateway forces them to break cover from the hedges.
Wood mice like to live in areas with plenty of cover –
brambles and bracken do nicely, and they are often found
scurrying about at speed in hedgerows, woods and gardens,
or tiptoeing carefully while they investigate. They tend to
migrate to some extent according to seasonal food supplies:
for example, they will move out of woodland in late spring
into arable crops, and then return to the woods in the
autumn for all those lovely nuts and fruit.

Both wood mice and yellow-necks are more than capable
of finding their way home from more than 300m (about
1,000ft) away, even twice as far. It is claimed that, if you
humanely trap either species and want to release them
elsewhere, you'll have to take them at least 2km (1¼ miles)
away or they'll soon be back. I know this from experience
with yellow-necks: I had a sudden invasion one year and
set up a humane trip-trap in the apple shed. Almost
immediately I caught a very angry and active (and smelly)
yellow-neck at 10 p.m. and I took it in the trap, struggling
and swearing at me all the way, for a walk some 300m down
the track before setting it free. It was back in the apple shed
before I was and kept on being caught. In the end, feeling
not a little foolish, I got into the car and furtively released it
a few kilometres down the road. Success.

The wood mouse breeds at almost any time from March

Wood mouse's footprints

to October, and even right through the winter if there is plenty of beechmast to keep it going. Typically it has four or five litters a year, with anything from three to eight or ten in each litter, and the young are ready to breed themselves by four months old. Wood mice make a nest of grass and leaves underground, often leaving a heap of excavated soil outside the burrow and disguising the entrance with stones and other debris. Yellow-necks are just as likely to nest in your loft or shed or in a convenient niche in the greenhouse, or they might even squat in a bird nestbox, but usually they, too, nest underground. Don't leave your wellies lying on their side in the garden shed . . .

Both species are theoretically nocturnal (though I often see them romping along the hedgerow in broad daylight) and are particularly active around dusk and dawn but don't much like being out and about in bright moonlight. Their tastes in food are broadly similar – fruit (yellow-necks will move mountains to reach stored apples), nuts, seedlings, buds (yummy camellias!), green shoots, snails, insect larvae, arthropods, fungi, moss, worms – whatever is about, really. Wood mice, like bank voles, eat rosehips but the mice eat the seeds and leave the flesh, whereas the vole eats the flesh and leaves the seeds; a wood mouse will eat both seeds and flesh of blackberries, hawthorn berries and elderberries, whereas the bank vole will only go for the flesh. Both mice are seed eaters; wood mice are more inclined to eat grass seeds than yellow-necks, which are cleverer at extracting beech nuts and will even eat the seeds in yew berries in winter. Both species like hazel nuts and gnaw a round hole in the side of the shell – you will see a ring of toothmarks around the hole, whereas a bank vole will leave a clean hole with no toothmarks and a dormouse will make a smooth hole with oblique toothmarks around the cut edge. Both mice adore acorns, and hoard them in big heaps.

In the garden, both species might have a go at your peas and beans, tomatoes, fruit of various kinds, bulbs and crocus flowers, and may also steal newly sown seeds, just like house mice. The trick is to sow your seeds when conditions are right for very quick germination, hopefully when the mice are so busy with other goodies that by the time they've found your seeds it's too late. Many gardeners still soak pea seeds in paraffin, or drizzle paraffin along the seed row, to deter would-be mouse thieves. The paraffin only affects the seeds; it gradually evaporates and will not taint the crop itself.

J Baxter of Lewes's tip for garden mice was to bury a large flower-pot upside down in the soil, with its base at ground level. A bait was placed at the bottom (he suggested corn) and the mice would eagerly go down through the pot's drainage hole, 'feast to their hearts' content and be unable

Yellow-necked mouse's footprints

again to procure their liberty'. Well, I should have thought any mouse would have the nous to dig its way to freedom.

Mouse in the house

The two species of mice that you might find in the house are house mice and yellow-necks. The former is by far the most common and the most troublesome, in that, like the rat, it is capable of spreading disease. Wood mice are less likely to come into the house than yellow-necks, and yellow-necks are mainly confined to areas close to woodland in parts of southern England and Wales.

House mice

House mice are much less welcome than yellow-necks, as they do present a health hazard. Their 'crimes' include not only eating your food but also spoiling it with urine (house mice tend to spread urine wherever they go) and droppings (up to fifty droppings a day per mouse), or by ripping open flour bags and suchlike. They also play havoc with insulation materials; exude a characteristically stale mousy smell; make paper nests in the linen cupboard; chew holes in the skirting-boards; leave dirty smears, footprints, runways, little mounds of faeces mixed up with urine and grease; and, more dangerously, chomp away merrily on electric wiring, which can be a serious fire hazard. They have an unnerving habit of streaking along the base of a wall like a silent shadow that you glimpse from the corner of your eye.

The house mouse is a little smaller than the wood mouse and weighs perhaps 17 to 20g (⅔ to ¼oz); it measures 7 to 9cm (2¾ to 3½in) excluding the tail, which is at least three-quarters as long again. It has smaller eyes and ears and its tail is more scaly and thicker than that of a wood mouse; its coat is a dull greyish-brown. It lives wherever humans live, though in the countryside it tends to be outnumbered by wood mice. It is athletic – running, jumping, climbing, tightrope-walking and swimming with ease (and probably skiing, riding and shooting, for all I know) – and sweetly loyal to a house once it has made itself at home, which it is quick to do as soon as there is a vacancy. The peak time for moving indoors is in late autumn, if yours are the the sort of mice that have been able to find easy living in the fields, woods and hedgerows throughout the summer.

House mice are social animals that live in colonies, with a well-established pecking order among males and a resentment of strangers. They are chatty animals, too, and if you hear high-pitched squeaking in your home, it is much more likely to be house mice than wood mice or yellow-necks. House mice are highly sensitive to sudden noises and to high frequencies, which is why sonic deterrents are increasingly being marketed for their control. These may or may not work – the track record of such devices is not yet long enough to prove their efficacy, and anyway the sounds might not penetrate into where the mice are. Their eyesight

House mouse

is better than that of wood mice but the senses of smell and taste are the essential ones when it comes to food.

House mice, like rats, eat almost anything – and certainly anything that a human would eat. An adult mouse eats about 4g (⅛oz) of food a day and they particularly favour cereal-based foods, fats (including dairy produce) and sweet things. They also eat fruit and greenstuffs to some extent, and perhaps insects, and might nibble at paper, plaster, glue and other odd materials. In the countryside they go for grain, grass seeds, weed seeds, plump insect larvae, fungi, plant roots and the occasional worm. They obtain most of their fluid intake from their food so do not necessarily need constant access to drinking water.

In towns, house mice are able to breed all year round, which might mean anything up to ten litters a year with perhaps four to eight young in each litter. The gestation period is nineteen to twenty days and the babies are suckled for up to three weeks. The mother builds a substantial nest for her babies out of whatever material she can shred up, tucking it under the floorboards, or behind the skirting-boards or in pipe ducts. The young are capable of mating when they are only five or six weeks old but their life expectancy at birth is only fourteen weeks in the wild.

Indoor yellow-necks

Sometimes yellow-necks seem to come into the loft in droves in the autumn and sound like the proverbial herd of elephants racing around up there. It is when they start dropping into the larder (if it's an old cottage) that the decision will probably be taken to call in the local pest-buster. Yellow-necks are increasingly attracting attention as house guests, though they have probably always taken advantage of country dwellings but were assumed to be house mice. They tend to make for the loft, or the space between the ground and first floors, and you are much less likely to glimpse them scuttling along the skirting-board inside a room in the style of a house mouse.

In one old Sussex cottage during the 1970s I had a few yellow-necks during the winter and you could always hear them pattering about in the night above the ground-floor ceiling. They made nests of old newspapers – very old newspapers: I took up some bedroom floorboards and discovered a nest made from a 1930s edition, though goodness knows how it got there.

One problem with yellow-necks is that they can chew through just about anything, including, for example, perforated zinc. They can also gnaw into a flat surface (most mice need an edge to start on) and can create a hole big enough to squeeze through in solid oak floorboards 1cm (½in) thick in less than a fortnight. This fact was recorded by the naturalist Arthur R Thompson who, in his book *Nature by Night* (1931), described his fascination with yellow-necks (which he called 'de Winton's mouse'). He kept several in captivity and was intrigued by their trick of throwing backward somersaults: they would leap on to the top of their hollow-log sleeping compartment and fling themselves off backwards, landing feet first on the floor. Then they would run round, jump up on to the log again and repeat the performance, time and time again for hours on end.

Thompson pointed out that the place to look for yellow-necks was in the kitchen gardens of large country houses, and in conservatories. They love hothouse peaches and nectarines, for example: first they eat the flesh of the fruit and then they open the stone and extract the kernel. It's alarming to think just how powerful their teeth and jaws must be to crack a peach stone.

Yellow-necks in the house are usually looking for snug quarters more than food, which makes it that much more difficult to dissuade them from coming indoors. Perhaps the best approach, though time-consuming, is to make sure that they have plenty of good accommodation elsewhere. It is also important not to attract them unwittingly with food; for example, don't leave birdfood lying around overnight (and remember that yellow-necks are good climbers and will easily reach hanging containers). They have a passion for apples, even the greenest of cookers, and orchard windfalls will soon draw them in. As for storing apples over the winter – forget it, unless your apple store is absolutely mouseproof. Yellow-necks, wood mice and house mice, it is said, can squeeze through any hole that is big enough for you to poke a ballpoint pen through. Many garden sheds are made of pine and in due course the knots fall out and produce the perfect entry hole for a mouse that can climb – which yellow-necks and house mice most certainly can.

You could try trapping yellow-necks, if you must. Poison is sometimes an alternative but you need to be absolutely sure that you find all the corpses before anything else does. You would do better to encourage predators and I still toy with the idea of taming a weasel to live in the loft.

Anti-mice

It has been found that a newly mated female house mouse will lose her fertilised eggs if within four days of the mating she is exposed to another male that she has not mated with; this means that she is instantly ready to mate again. There is a possibility that this reaction is triggered by certain proteins in the new male's urine. So perhaps some bottled mouse pee could be used as a morning-after potion? Or would it simply make the situation worse? House mice are at their most active around dusk and before dawn; in theory their peak times are 8 to 10 p.m. and 4 to 6 a.m. and they are basically creatures of the night, when it's safer to be about the house. They have numerous predators, including barn owls, stoats, weasels, rats and of course cats and humans. Cats (and weasels and ferrets) are good mousers but with cats it is so often just a game, rather than a serious hunt-to-eat, and they frequently release their prey, or even bring it into the house when it was perfectly happy to live outside. So maybe cats aren't always the answer.

J Baxter of Lewes's advice on rats or mice living behind the wainscots was to drive them out by fumigation: common salt in a tablespoon with sulphuric acid poured on top to create 'so much suffocating gas . . . as to cause their almost immediate expulsion'. Goodness knows what it did to the person handling the mixture!

Other means of control have tried the greatest of brains for centuries and all sorts of ingenious mousetraps have been invented. House mice might initially pause when a new object like a trap suddenly intrudes across their regular run (which is where it needs to be placed) but, unlike rats, which won't go near this new thing for maybe 48 hours, mice quickly become curious and investigate it. A good trap bait is peanut butter, which can't be snatched away by a cunning mouse. And cunning they certainly are. They soon become 'bait-shy', or clever enough to steal that nice piece of cheese or chocolate without getting snapped to eternity in a back-breaker trap. Your local council's environmental health department will probably be more successful with mouse control than you are.

If you insist on using poisons, you might do better with the contact method than with bait. Place the poison along a regular run where the mouse will brush against it in passing; it will then lick the stuff off during grooming and ingest it. Poisoning should be the last resort, partly because many of the poisons present a risk to household pets and even children and partly because there is very often a major problem with corpses. If the mouse dies under your floorboards, you will know about it when the stink starts to permeate the house. If it dies outside, you will constantly be fretting about what other animal might have consumed the corpse. All corpses should be burnt, or at least deeply buried. Don't flush them down the loo.

At least with trapping you know exactly where the body is and can dispose of it tidily, but inevitably with trapping there can be some very unpleasant mistakes when the mouse is mutilated but not killed instantly. One of my least favourite childhood memories is of living in an old cottage in which I could hear the mice scampering nightly behind the wood panelling on the wall right by my bed; but worse was that little thud and squeak as the trap's sprung metal bar crashed down across their tiny bodies. Worse still was when the trap didn't kill them outright but caught them by the leg and you could hear them desperately throwing themselves and the trap around in an attempt to escape.

So, as ever, seek to deter rather than kill. It is said that mice can't stand the smell of peppermint essence (douse it on cotton wool) or, strangely, watercress, which you can hang in bunches near the food you are trying to protect.

Above all, deterrence means scrupulous hygiene within the home and making absolutely certain that mice have no means of access to anything remotely edible. If they can't find food, they'll leave home and find somewhere more amenable. Look for possible entry points, which will be numerous – what about that small gap in the outside wall around the kitchen wastepipe, for example? Any mouse can find its way into the house – perhaps climbing into the loft (they can be brilliant wall-scalers, especially with the help of virginia creeper, ivy or roses) or through airbrick holes to find their way into cavity walls – and once inside it is no problem for a mouse to chew through woodwork and gain access to where it really wants to be. To make a larder or kitchen mouseproof, let alone an entire house, is quite a challenge, but you can do it! You're more intelligent and ingenious than a little mouse! Aren't you?

House mouse's footprints

Nuisance Cats

This chapter deals with your neighbours – not the humans but their animals, specifically cats that use your garden as a toilet or chase your birds. Wild cats, even the elusive panthers that might be stalking the countryside, are beyond the scope of this book (contact the police or your local council's wildlife officer for help); so are the wild boar and goats that have become feral in some areas. There is just the faintest possibility that your intruders are wallabies: in the 1940s red-necked wallabies escaped and established feral populations in the Peak District and in the Sussex Weald, but you are more likely to see them as road casualties than in your garden, if at all.

If the neighbourly problem is, say, persistently barking dogs or a dog that keeps coming into your garden for any reason, that is something you and the dog owner will have to sort out between you. The dog owner is obliged to keep the dog under control. With farm livestock, again it is up to the owner to fence them in rather than up to you to fence them out (though those with commoners' rights will claim it is the other way around).

119

Cat owners, however, have no such obligation with their pets. Cats, their owners always claim, cannot be controlled anyway and therefore have the right to roam where they please and do as they please. It is an arguable point but, legally, they seem to be right and, legally, you as the offended party may not take pot-shots at cats; you may not deliberately set your dog to chasing cats; and you may not resort to cat-napping.The main problems caused by other people's cats are digging up or scent-marking your garden, hunting your birds, caterwauling in cat fights, and perhaps boldly coming into your house to make themselves at home on a sunny bed or to scratch your furniture.

PUBLIC TOILETS

Cat scats in your garden are not only unpleasant; they also carry diseases that can be passed to humans, especially children. That includes, for example, toxoplasmosis, which is one reason why you should wear rubber gloves when gardening and should make quite sure that the children's sandpit is covered so that cats (and dogs) can't use it as a toilet.

Cats using the garden as a toilet are looking for some nice dry, workable soil in which they can bury their scats. A newly dug area is ideal for a cat and usually that means the vegetable patch or flower beds, especially newly sown seedbeds. This really is the fault of the cat owner, who should have trained their cat to use a litter tray like any other civilised cat. All sorts of methods have been tried against cats that insist on soiling in gardens and many of them don't work at all. One of the simplest, if rather labour-intensive, is to keep any bare soil moist, because cats don't like getting their paws muddy when they are performing this important daily function. So if you see someone furtively watering a bare vegetable patch last thing at night, they are probably plagued by cats.

Another trick, if the area is not too large, is to make bare surfaces uncomfortable for cats by spreading something prickly like holly leaves or chopped gorse over the soil or even scrunched-up eggshells (as you would against slugs), or covering seedbeds with garden fleece, or dotting the area with short vertical sticks so that there is no room for a cat to perform. You could try criss-crossing the area with prickly stems from roses or brambles, pegged down, or try to fool the cat by leaving a bicycle inner-tube lying around pretending to be a snake – though just as many cats are likely to see a snake as an interesting hunting challenge as to be alarmed by it.

Then there are smells that cats don't seem to like: mothballs (dogs don't like those either), citrus peel, pepper dust, eucalyptus oil (soaked into teabags), or lion or tiger poo from the local zoo, which is sometimes sold in tidy pellets that won't pong you out. There are numerous commercial anti-cat pongs but some of them need to be replaced when it rains and some of them make no difference at all to individual cats.

Cat scats dropped on the lawn are a different matter: they are usually a signal from a tomcat telling other cats that he is boss around here. Neutered toms and females prefer to bury the evidence.

ON THE HUNT

The other problem with cats is that they are born hunters and their hunting might include your garden birds. Some of the deterrents already mentioned might help but above all you need to place bird-feeding areas so that they are at least three cat-sized bounds away from cat cover. Any low branches on nearby shrubbery should be trimmed out so that cats cannot hide underneath. With your own cats, you could try belling them but you will need to fit two bells to the collar (any cat worth its salt is capable of keeping one bell silent). Or you could go modern and fit a collar that bleeps when the cat moves.

Some owners assume that a well-fed cat will not hunt but in fact eating and hunting are separate instincts. Even a full-up cat still has the urge to hunt, if that is the type of cat it is. Also, the fed cat is more likely just to play with its prey, rather than killing it outright, which is no fun for the prey. If it is your own cat, you could try feeding it or playing with it at just the sort of time it might have been thinking of going hunting, so that it decides home is a better place to be, or you could use the distraction technique, interrupting the cat at the stalking stage with a loud noise but making sure it connects the disturbance with its own act and not with you.

KEEP 'EM OUT

You could try to deter cats from coming into the garden, or certain areas of it, in the first place – perhaps with the help of prickly hedges or by spraying dilute surgical spirit on walls and fences where the cats come in or smearing the walls with something like tree grease. It probably won't deter a determined cat if the garden itself remains attractive for one reason or another.

There are many cat-scaring devices on the market to keep cats out of the garden, whether as seedbed diggers or as bird catchers or general nuisance. They include motion-activated water sprinklers, originally invented in Canada to scare off deer but equally applicable to cats, dogs or rabbits (and they would keep the soil nice and damp at the same time). The newest aids are sonic devices that emit high-frequency sounds, either constantly or when a cat (or some other animal) breaks across an infra-red beam. Some scientific studies say they make no difference at all to some cats – especially white ones, which tend to be deaf. White cats, incidentally, are very helpful to wildlife: any bird that you are feeding in the garden will spot a white cat on the stalk long before it is near enough to be a threat.

With almost anything you try, be it noises, smells or discomfort, something that would deter one cat will be ignored by another. Maybe the answer is to get a cat or cats of your own, who will establish the garden as their territory and see off intruders, with luck. Your own cats, of course, will be properly trained, and you might even give them a private corner in the garden for toileting, complete with cat litter.

When you are training your own cat not to defecate in the wrong place, one of the methods is to distract it every time (but it must be every time) it tries to use that place. Cats don't like being interrupted in these serious matters. But the cat must not connect the distraction directly with you, or it will simply learn not to do it while you are around. Hence the use of remote-controlled devices that fire off water or make a loud noise. Nor do cats like being watched in the act and I wonder idly whether a false pair of eyes might do the trick. Similar ideas could be adapted for the neighbour's cat.

Sometimes the 'home' cat suffers the immense indignity of alien cats not only invading the garden but having the nerve to march straight indoors through the catflap. This is truly demoralising for the resident cat and I have known perfectly sensible cats who have been reduced to shivering wimps by such intrusions, or, if there is more than one cat in the family, have taken it out on one of their home mates by way of displacement aggression. In these cases the answer is to fit the home cats with special electronic collars that control the opening of the catflap so that no strangers can strut into the kitchen and make themselves at home.

You could get a dog, to make the neighbours' cats feel unwelcome, but dogs are humanised and tend to be active in the day, whereas intruding cats are more likely to be active by night. Another domestic daytime deterrent is geese, which are highly and noisily protective of their territory, though they do have the drawback of chasing postmen and of leaving more of a mess of poo than any neighbour's cat. Geese have the added advantage of destroying ground elder by persistent grazing, but close neighbours might object to their cackling.

People who personally lie in wait for cats so that they can chase them off will find that the cats have an uncanny knack of knowing when you are not at home and taking advantage of your absence. If you are really feeling so stressed by invading cats that you are lying in wait for them, it is time to contact the Cat Protection helpline for new ideas: call 01403 221900.

Birds

Most of the problems people have with birds involve fouling with droppings, stealing food, damaging plants, damaging buildings, or presenting a health hazard. Most of the remedies involve scaring them away by means of sounds or sights, or simply removing whatever it is that attracts them. Reducing the population by killing is very much the last resort and, as ever, if the attraction remains, other birds will come in to take the place of the culled victims.

Writing two centuries ago, J Baxter of Lewes pointed out that sparrows, for example, fed on insects as well as seeds and that in many cases they were 'a benefit rather than an injury . . . by destroying wire-worm and many other insects'. He credited crows and rooks likewise; although many decribed them as 'a most destructive race' and practised all-out slaughter on them, he himself thought that the corvids did an excellent job of leaving fields 'better, cleaner, and freer from the grub and weeds' and should be treated with more respect. I begin to warm to Baxter!

GARDEN GUESTS

Bullfinches

Typical complaints include those beautiful, plump, rosy-chested bullfinches that strip buds from fruit trees and flowering shrubs. It looks like vandalism, but a fruit tree can afford to lose as much as two-thirds of all its buds without the yield of fruit being significantly affected. Indeed, there might be benefits from the bullfinches' pruning: the yield might actually be improved, or at least the individual fruits might be bigger and better, as the tree will not be dissipating its energy into too many buds.

There is very little point in trying out some of the old remedies against bullfinches, most of which were diabolical and involved traps. Baxter said: 'It is too much the practice with gardeners to destroy or frighten away the feathered race from orchards, whether in blossom or in fruit – a system most injudicious when we find that the birds which frequent orchards, particularly bullfinches, during the bloom, are not only seeking their own proper food, but are benefiting the proprietor by the destruction of numberless insects, "the worm i' the bud," that lie in the yet unfolded blossoms, where they had been deposited until the warmth which swells the buds acts upon them likewise, bringing forth a most numerous race of caterpillars, ready to annihilate the early hopes of the owner. In fact, it is a question whether the destruction, committed by birds upon the seed, is not more than counterbalanced by the essential service which they render by extirpating the larvae of some of the most destructive insects.' Do you get the feeling that Baxter was ahead of his time?

Corvids

Various members of the corvid family are also on many people's not-wanted list. There is a strong suspicion, sometimes valid, that magpies, jays, crows and so on are stealing eggs from birds' nests and taking the nestlings as well. Magpies, some people swear, even steal eggs from cartons left on the doorstep by the milkman and will peck at the putty that is supposed to be keeping your glass in place. It is claimed that these corvids are on the increase with the decline of gamekeeping (keepers used to be ruthless in killing them, to protect their gamebird eggs and chicks). In desperation in country areas some people set live traps for magpies, which involves putting another magpie inside a cage as a lure to catch one of its conspecifics. But then what do you do with the trapped bird? Kill it, they cry. Well, maybe, but be careful: you might suddenly find you like magpies. In the old days quite a few cottagers would keep a caged magpie or jay as a pet and teach it all sorts of tricks. Some of the corvids are excellent mimics and were much easier to come by than parrots if you liked that sort of thing.

Sparrow hawks

People who enjoy feeding small birds in the winter are often deeply upset when the feeding flocks are raided by what is most likely to be a sparrow hawk. From the hawk's point of view, you are simply feeding the hawk, which is most generous of you, by attracting a crowd of its prey to one point and letting them get distracted by all that peanut-bashing. Actually, there are always birds on the alert for hawks in areas where there are local birds of prey, and very often you will hear the immediately recognisable alarm calls and chatters that cause every bird in the garden to disappear instantly into the nearest cover. Sparrow hawks make many raids but are only occasionally successful, and you will not notice much of a depletion in bird numbers. And hawks are hawks – they are carnivores, they need meat, they must catch birds in order to live and to feed their young.

There is very little you can or should do about it; just sit back and admire the close-up sight of a vaguely disgruntled hawk perched on the pergola, having missed its intended victims and knowing that every bird in the garden is aware of its presence so that it has no chance of success. They are beautiful birds and I wouldn't be without them. The only steps I would take are to ensure that there is always plenty of cover for the prey birds close to the feeding stations. For example, a thick tangle of thorny climbing roses will thwart any hawk. You could also try the trick of pushing tall bamboo canes into the ground around the bird table at random, the theory being that they will distract the hawk long enough to give birds a chance to flee.

Wood pigeons and doves

Pigeons and doves are not favourites with some people. Wood pigeons and those beautiful white doves raid all sorts of crops, from grains to vegetables; collared doves swipe all the birdfood and their persistent cooing is irritating to some people. But surely nobody could ever be irritated by the soft summer sound of turtle doves, if you should be lucky enough to hear them? To keep out pigeons and collared doves, you can devise a system of cages to protect the birdfood, making sure that the 'welcome' birds still have access but the bigger birds are kept out.

Defending the vegetable patch

Farmers usually go for noisy bangers and flashers that are set off at intervals as bird scarers, or shoot crop-raiding pigeons on a regular basis. After long ancestral experience, pigeons are very wary of the sight of people with guns and will often avoid even a cut-out silhouette of a man with a raised gun (try that one in your vegetable patch). They and other birds are also naturally suspicious of bird of prey and so cottagers protecting their cabbages would make an artificial hawk and string it up on a very long pole to hover above the trees. Old Baxter's idea for the vegetable patch was to take a slender hazel rod about 1.8 to 2.5m (6 to 8ft) long and push it into the ground at a slant, attaching a hanging cord at the tip, to which was fixed a potato 'stuck full of feathers of different colours', suspended about 30 to 40cm (12 to 15in) above the ground.

Unless you have the services of someone with nothing better to do than stand around with a bird-scaring rattle all day long, the traditional scarecrow has its place in the garden and you could try your own modern version. Devise something that moves unpredictably and constantly so that the birds can never settle down comfortably to the business of seed-pecking. Try things that sparkle, things that hum, things that flash or flutter, unexpectedly bright colours, strange patterns, sudden noises – look for inspiration in organic gardening catalogues but don't always believe the claims. Try the predator scam: if you can't make a hawk 'kite', float a carefully chosen helium-filled balloon above the vulnerable area. Its position needs to be changed frequently and at random or the birds will soon suss that it is not for real.

You could also try keeping birds out by netting your vegetables and fruit, but do take care if you are using plastic netting. Young songbirds easily become entangled if the netting is a bit loose and I learnt my lesson long ago on finding a spotted, newly fledged robin dangling dead, head down, with one leg caught in the mesh. Another old gardener's trick was to use strands of black thread to keep various birds away from newly sown seeds or seedlings, but this is a bad idea. I have seen a perfectly innocent thrush caught up in thread when all it was doing was searching for snails, like the good gardener's friend that the thrush always is. There is a commercial alternative that looks like a huge cobweb: it is made from cellulose and you drape it over fruit trees or above soft fruit and vegetables. It is light enough not to ensnare the birds, but they should be deterred from finding their way through. In the old days, gardeners would cover newly seeded vegetable patches with mats or old fishing-nets until the seedlings began to sprout.

Taste aversion is a more complicated technique and is based on finding a taste that a bird dislikes and applying it to whatever you want to protect. If you are really serious, link the bad taste with a visual message. For example, birds avoid black-and-yellow-striped insects in case they sting; they also avoid anything the colour and pattern of a ladybird because they know a ladybird is not good to eat. There are many patterns in nature known as warning coloration: they alert birds that this thing is going to make them feel unwell, as it did the first time they tried it. (This technique also works with rodents.) If you are inventing your own warning coloration, it would have to be teamed with taste aversion

---

Whatever tricks you use to scare birds away, change them often as birds soon grow used to them. Learn as much as you can about bird behaviour: exploit their normal audible or visual alarm signals and their alarm postures on the one hand, and imitate their predators on the other, bearing in mind that they are more likely to worry about a moving predator than a static cat hidden in the bushes unseen.

but that would mean teaching every bird in the garden by experience. Stick to what all birds already recognise!

WATER GUESTS

Garden ponds are vital for wildlife but of course they also attract those that would be predators of the wildlife in the pond, including ornamental fish. A particular culprit is the heron or, on a lake rather than a pond, perhaps a cormorant. With cormorants, try stretching wires across the water 15 to 25m (50 to 80ft) apart. With herons, scale the distance down and stretch netting over the pond or just under the water. Think heron: a heron prefers a gently sloping bank, so you could make your banks steep (except that most of the wildlife using the pond also likes a shallow slope). Try ringing the pond with two wires or cords, the first about 25cm (10in) above ground level and the second 10cm (4in) higher, so that the heron finds access to the water too difficult. Some people install mock herons, on the presumption that an incoming heron will not intrude on a present heron's territory, but if that mock heron is always in exactly the same place and position, any intelligent incomer will realise that it isn't flesh-and-feather.

HOUSE GUESTS

City pigeons and gulls

In cities, feral pigeons can create havoc by roosting on buildings; the birds are known to carry various transmittable diseases, and the avalanche of accumulated droppings looks unsightly, erodes the masonry and blocks the gutters, especially when mixed with feathers, discarded nesting material and corpses.

The authorities try a wide range of deterrents against pigeons and starlings: plastic-covered wire netting, strands of wire strained just above where they perch, creating sloping bevels over flat surfaces so that they are less perchable, broadcasting distress calls as the birds come in to roost, encouraging a resident falcon, fluttering strips of PVC from the eaves (very elegant), painting surfaces with fruit-tree banding grease or some other jelly-like substance (not to be recommended, as the stuff can stick to their feathers), applying metal spikes with a backing strip rather like some dimininutive anti-tank mat (undesirably dangerous for the birds), gruesome measures that include the use of chemo-sterilants or stupefacients (don't even think of them) or using ultrasonic devices which now seem to be marketed as the absolute deterrent against all pests. Well, maybe, but you will find that most birds are unable to hear frequencies higher than those that are audible to humans.

Gulls seem to have opted for nesting on buildings for the first time around about the 1930s – especially herring gulls. It began in coastal areas but now seems to be spreading into urban areas. The gulls have big strong beaks and can cheerfully rip away bits of your flat roof or tear out loose material. They are very vocal, raucously so, and, rather like starlings, they strut about with what appears to be arrogance. They instantly steal any bread or scraps put out for other birds; quite often they scavenge on nearby rubbish tips and transport some of their findings to their resting place on your roof. They produce a prodigious amount of very messy droppings, and also gobbets of regurgitated food, which can disfigure the roof or land on parked cars and people below. What is worse, a nesting pair of gulls is quite likely to mob humans anywhere near the nest, in order to protect the young, and this can be quite frightening, especially for children or the elderly.

Is there a practical do-it-yourself answer to gulls? Local councils in seaside areas will be well used to complaints and might have an idea or two. Again, the problem is that as long as your roof remains attractive and even if you get rid of one lot of gulls, there are plenty more queuing up for such a desirable site. In the meantime, you can only do your best to protect anything below roofline from their droppings, or perhaps you could deliberately collect the guano and sell it as fertiliser.

Migrants

House bird 'pests' are much easier to live with, though I might be prejudiced. I don't mind the dumpy little partridges that roost on the roof now and then, talking away to each other and leaving a guano trail from the ridge. I don't mind the swallows – they are hugely welcome, that wonderful promise of summer, and I was truly flattered when they at last began to plaster mud from the pond against the tile-hanging of the cottage; I didn't even mind the constant splattering when the young were old enough to stick their backsides over the edge of the nest and let loose. I knew they would be gone all too soon and it doesn't take long to hose down the terrace beneath.

The same is true for house martins. If you are really worried about your pristine car down below, it should be easy enough to rig up a protective sheet or timber to catch the droppings before they come anywhere near ground level. Alternatively, you could deter them from nesting by stretching small-mesh garden netting tautly over vulnerable areas, or making a loose string lattice, long enough to hang below the nesting area with the loose ends left fluttering, to deter them from flying in. But why do that? It's only for a few weeks, after all, and if you stop to think about the staggering distances that 'your' birds have flown to reach your house, surely you can't begrudge them a temporary nest? And what about all those midges and gnats that they will be snapping up for you?

Starlings and house sparrows

Two-faced human that I am, I used to mind the starlings that were in residence when I first came here. They nested under the eaves all over the place, scuttling about noisily, ripping out roofing felt, making holes in old fascia boards, dislodging tiles, forever dropping their babies down the cavity between the outside walls (impossible to retrieve), sitting on top of the Rayburn chimney ejecting birdcherry stones that rattled into the cooker, and sometimes getting themselves trapped down the flue (which meant a major rescue operation). Their nests were a great mess of plant material, feathers and whatnot but then they would go and do something enchanting like decorating them with forget-me-nots. Sometimes I loved to hear the starlings chattering and arguing and whistling and mimicking telephones and other bird calls; sometimes it drove me crazy, and quite unreasonably I also found their apparent arrogance aggravating, strutting about on the lawn and bullying the smaller birds on the bird table. Yet their plumage is gorgeous.

Starlings are quite new to house-squatting. They are by nature cliff nesters and it wasn't until the nineteenth century that they starting building up the enormous urban roosts that have become so common. In those situations they can be quite a serious problem, mainly because in such large numbers there is a mountain of droppings beneath the roost. In quantity, rather than being a fertiliser, the droppings can kill grass and trees. If they rain down on the road, they can create a dangerously slippery surface for traffic. So, yes, in towns massed starlings are a problem.

There are measures you can take to dissuade house-nesters if they become intolerable. There is absolutely no point in slaughtering them, because, as ever in nature, if a habitat is desirable, someone else will soon move in. The aim is to make that habitat less desirable, which usually means lack of food or lack of nesting and roosting sites. An old country way of deterring starlings was to attach small weights to strings about 35cm (14in) long and hang them about 10 to 15cm (4 to 6in) apart to prevent a direct flight approach to nesting sites by starlings, but allowing access by the martins.

Eventually my starlings left me because of building work that included patching up weak points, which starlings had probably been exploiting ever since this Victorian cottage was built. Although rather relieved that they had moved on, I also felt enormously guilty. That was several years ago, before there began to be reports that starling numbers were seriously declining. I seldom see them in the garden now and feel even more guilty that I have probably, like so many other people, contributed to their demise. Perhaps I should have reached a compromise. Funnily enough, I do miss their vocal repertoire, their mimicry and their sheer lust for life.

Some people feel the same ambivalence about house sparrows. I used to live in a 'sparrow cottage' and never

Birds in the room

Very occasionally a bird might find itself indoors by mistake and will panic, which means it will squit wherever it goes. To encourage it out again, open just one window or outside door and darken all other windows with curtains or blinds. The bird will fly towards the only daylight. If it is an uncertain fledgling, it will probably cower in a corner somewhere. Very, very gently, cover it with your hand or with a soft lightweight cloth: all birds (and most animals) become calm when their eyes are covered. Then you can pick it up, ever so gently, with both hands so that it is still 'in the dark'. Take it outside and put it somewhere safe from cats.

Swallows and their relatives have a habit of swooping about the room at ceiling level, never quite low enough to find all those open windows. Again, if you darken all except one opening, they will quickly escape. That, after all, is what a bird wants – to be free and to get back to the world it knows, outside.

tired of their cheerful chirruping, their sociability and their cheekiness. I didn't mind the fact that they instantly shredded yellow crocuses, never even trying the trick of growing these near lavender to deter such vandalism. In my present surroundings sparrows are oddly rare, mainly because of changes in farming practice that have affected so many other grain-eating birds. The local farmers tend to plough straight after harvest, so there are no winter pickings in the stubble for birds as there always used to be.

Farmers also do their best to eradicate weeds and insects by spraying their crops and it is hardly surprising that farmland birds are vanishing from the countryside.

Slipperies

None of the reptiles (snakes and lizards) and amphibians (toads, frogs and newts) described in this chapter can really be called a pest, though one of them is venomous and there are a few alien invaders that could become local nuisances.

Britain is not well off for reptiles and amphibians. There are only six native species of reptile and six of amphibian. Several of these species are rare or declining and even the more common ones are under threat from loss of habitat as the nation keeps increasing its concrete-and-tarmac grip on the land and tidying up all the usefully unkempt and damp places that these animals need. In addition, many people buy exotic reptiles and amphibians, then decide that they have grown too big or the children are bored by them, so dump them in the great outdoors to fend for themselves. In some cases these exotics have thrived and by virtue of size and aggression have begun to displace the natives, or even to gobble them up.

TOADS, FROGS AND NEWTS

The amphibian species of Britain are the common toad, the rare natterjack toad, the common frog, the great crested newt, the palmate newt and the common or smooth newt. The common toad and common frog are widespread, but in recent years even these once ubiquitous creatures have suffered population crashes – partly due to environmental problems and partly due to disease. The natterjack is rare and very local, mainly restricted to sandy heathland and coastal dunes. Smooth newts are widespread in lowland areas; palmate newts are common on heaths and uplands; and the great crested or warty newt is widespread but far from common.

The nature of amphibians is that they spend part of their lives in water: that is where they mate and where they lay their eggs (spawn) and pass the first stage of their lives as tadpoles. It is also where some of them hibernate in winter. Otherwise, most of them spend most of their lives on land but both their aquatic and their terrestrial habitats are rapidly disappearing or being disrupted.

Hoppers and crawlers

To tell what is a frog and what is a toad, watch it on the move. Frogs are athletic and basically hop or leap, while toads are rather squat and reluctant to move but basically crawl (or run if they are natterjacks). Frogs have smooth, moist skin; toads have dry, warty skin. Natterjacks are smaller than common toads and have a characteristic yellow stripe down their backs. Adult frogs and toads eat plenty of beetles, bugs, ants and woodlice; both also eat slugs and snails but frogs are fonder of them than are toads, and toads eat more ants than do frogs. Frogs will also eat butterflies and moths.

Common frog

Any gardener would be delighted to have a resident toad in the greenhouse and should welcome frogs and toads anywhere in the garden. They can be encouraged to come and stay if you have the right kind of pond for them. This should be a wildlife pond (rather than a formal one), with a gently sloping bank for easy access into and out of the water, and water of the right depth for egg-laying – shallow areas (maybe 15cm or 6in) for a frog, preferably in a small pond, and a little deeper (20 to 30 cm, or 8 to 12in) for a toad, preferably in a large pond. The tadpoles eat algae and microscopic animals in the water but they also eat larger dead animals, including other dead or ailing tadpoles. Tadpoles are eaten by just about every meat-eater that can catch them – from water beetles and dragonfly nymphs to newts and birds.

In these early years of the new millennium, the common frog is in bad trouble in Britain. An American viral disease commonly known as 'red leg' has been rampaging through

Common toad

the native frog population here and 90 per cent of the frogs that catch it will die, covered in sores along their legs and bodies that can be so severe that feet or limbs are lost. It is quite possible that the disease has already claimed the lives of a million British frogs in southern England and Wales. As if that wasn't enough, frogs and toads are also being weakened by eating slugs that have been poisoned by gardeners and farmers. Innumerable tiny froglets and toadlets, newly emerged from tadpole life in the pond, are mown to smithereens by gardeners who fail to see them in the grass. On top of all that, they are being eaten by a large and greedy alien from North America: the bullfrog, sold by garden centres and pet shops to stock garden ponds during the 1980s. This big bully likes nothing better than a mouthful of British frog.

As for the 'nuisance' value of native frogs and toads, it is limited to croaking during the mating season (from February for frogs, through March for common toads until as late as early June for natterjack toads, whose voices can carry a mile or more) and to swarming across gardens and roads to reach the ancestral breeding ponds. The croaking might keep you awake for a few nights but to most people it's a delightful and evocative sound.

Countless toads, in particular, are slaughtered on the roads at this vital breeding stage: they have a very strong urge to return to the pond in which they were born, even if it is a mile away, and will do so regardless of the fact that, say, a new housing estate has been built on the site or a motorway slashes across their route. Toads tend to make for their ponds in mass surges (frogs are less crowd-minded) and that, combined with their slow locomotion, invariably means large numbers of squashed toads on the roads.

In self-defence (not that it's any good against a vehicle), toads in danger basically sit still and hope nobody notices them, or in the face of a potential predator they might puff themselves up and stand on tiptoe to look bigger, which fools nobody. If they are surprised, they might empty their bladders, which harms nobody but the liquid has a faint smell, or if they are caught and squeezed, they release their secret weapon: a sticky white secretion exuded from their warts. A dog that has picked up a toad will promptly start foaming at the mouth and quickly spit out the offending and offended toad. The dog will probably be sick, and occasionally might show signs of temporary local paralysis, but it will have learnt its lesson and will never grab another toad.

Apart from the butch bullfrog, there are one or two other aliens at loose in the wild but they tend to be localised. The edible frog was introduced from France and Belgium in the 1830s and remains basically a Londoner or an East Anglian, with isolated colonies elsewhere, while the big marsh frog imported originally from Hungary in the 1930s loiters in Kent and neighbouring parts of Sussex (and very noisy they can be too). Then there is the small European tree frog, which is also very noisy; herpetologist Trevor Beebee has described the sound as a cross between a dog barking and a duck quacking. There is said to be only a tiny population by a single pond in the New Forest but I wonder about Wiltshire. Back in the late 1940s I remember climbing into a high garden tree and finding what I thought was a bird's nest – I had the fright of my life when a small green frog jumped out of it. As for toads, there are a few small midwife toads in Bedfordshire and a few of the secretive and wholly aquatic South African clawed toad on the Isle of Wight and in Wales.

Amphibians with tails

You are more likely to see an adult newt diving in a pond than wandering about on the land. When I made a small wildlife pond in my garden, I was delighted that some

Male palmate newt – with webbed back feet (the female has no webbing) and a much lower, plainer crest than other species

smooth newts discovered it in the very first season and took up residence. Common and palmate newts are small – between about 7 and 10cm (2¾ and 4in); the great crested might grow up to about 16cm (6in) and needs a deeper pond.

Once they have found a good pond, newts tend to stay in or near it, in contrast to wandering frogs and toads. They are enchanting animals to watch if you have time to linger. Their tadpoles look like miniature versions of the adults and often stay in their pond of birth until the next spring. They won't be mature until they are two or even three years old, if they survive that long (fish are the main predators). Tadpoles and adults are carnivores, eating anything aquatic, including frog tadpoles; the adults, coming out of the pond in midsummer, hunt at night for worms and slugs. There is no way a newt could be labelled as a pest.

REPTILES

There is huge prejudice against reptiles and you can blame it all on a mixture of folklore and primeval fears. People see a snake, or even the suspicion of one, and they instantly jump back, shudder and have a strong urge to bash it to smithereens. There are so many misconceptions about them. As a child I happened to be in the front row at a circus one day and an enormous snake was brought over to me. 'Go on, stroke it,' I was told. With great distaste, I put out a tentative hand, expecting to meet something slimy and horrible. To my great surprise, the skin wasn't slimy at all.

As well as snakes and lizards, the reptiles include the chelonians: tortoises, turtles and terrapins. None of them is native to Britain but you might come across ones that have escaped or been released into the wild.

Reptiles have a problem with temperature: they need to absorb heat from their surroundings. If it is too cold, they remain torpid, which is why they all disappear into hibernation during the winter. One of the nicest signs of spring is to see a reptile basking in the sun, getting ready for action; however, this is also when they are at their most vulnerable.

Reptiles don't breed until they are at least two years old (depending on species), and most of them will have perished before reaching breeding age. Some of them give birth to live young; some of them lay eggs in true dinosaur style.

Lizards

Lizards, lounging in the sun and well camouflaged against the stones (they can adjust their skin tones to melt into the background), might startle you with their sudden scuttling, but they do no harm at all. They don't have any means of defence other than shedding their tails if something grabs at them. Apart from humans and their vehicles, lizard predators include just about anything that fancies an easy mouthful of meat.

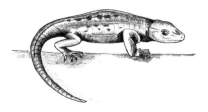

Common lizard

There are three native lizards in Britain: the dainty little common lizard (which is widespread and adaptable), the sturdier sand or hedge lizard (which is rare and very localised) and the slim, legless, polished-looking slow-worm, which is widespread and often mistaken for a snake. As a child I would have pet slow-worms, which was probably rather unfair on them but gave me much pleasure. It still gives me a thrill to come across slow-worms by an old stone wall and they really do seem to respond to you and be less shy than other reptiles. You need to be very gentle when handling them: their Latin name is *Anguis fragilis*, because it is so easy for them to lose their tail when danger threatens. Female slow-worms are usually pregnant for a whole year or more.

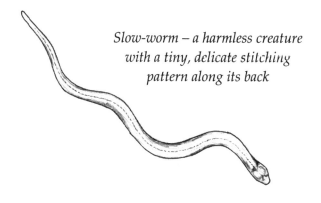

Slow-worm – a harmless creature with a tiny, delicate stitching pattern along its back

There are a few aliens in the land as well, including two European species that have escaped from captivity: the green lizard and the wall lizard. The exotic lizard group includes iguanas, geckoes, skinks, 'dragons', gila monsters and the like.

Lizards are hunters of invertebrates and patrol regular routes in their patch. They pounce on things like spiders, flying ant swarms (and ant eggs), crickets, wasps and other insects, stunning them and swallowing them more or less whole. Slow-worms are excellent slug controllers in the garden and they also eat earthworms, spiders, ant larvae, caterpillars, small snails and assorted insects. Every gardener should have at least one slow-worm and a toad.

The lizard family have a host of predators, including foxes, badgers, weasels, hedgehogs, snakes and birds of prey, and young lizards are swiped readily by shrews, corvids, thrushes, blackbirds, robins and even frogs and toads.

Snakes

No, don't shudder; don't look away. You really can learn to love snakes. It's just that they move so suddenly and they slither and you know all about Adam and Eve.

In Britain, all of the native snakes are protected: it must be stressed that it is illegal to kill or harm them in any way, and that there is no need to do so. It is also illegal to sell them. The three native British species are the very rare smooth snake, the delightful grass snake and the shy adder or viper. All our native snakes are scared of you and just want to be left alone: all of them would prefer to slip out of sight, and they all have excellent camouflage to remain unseen.

Only the adder has any venom, but this is not strong enough to do more than irritate. The venom is designed for killing little things, not great big humphing ones like humans. An adder can only get its bite round something very small. There is a possibility that an adder might bite a nosy dog or cat, and the animal will not feel very well afterwards, but it is highly unlikely to die from an adder bite (though it is sensible to take it straight to a vet). As for humans, in the hundred years from 1876 to 1976, only about a dozen people in Britain died from adder bites, and all of them were just unlucky enough to be hypersensitive, in the way that some people can die from a bee sting.

Adders are not in the least aggressive. The only time they might bite is in self-defence if they can't escape – they'd much rather you hadn't seen them at all and their urge is simply to slither into hiding. However, when they are warming up, especially just after a long winter's hibernation, they are rather stupefied and might not have heard you coming. That is when they might suddenly find you about to tread on them and so they might bite in self-defence. Even then, their 'strike' reach is no more than about 15cm (6in). If you do get bitten, the first rule is to remain calm – you are not going to die and you'll probably find the bite is no worse than a sting. You should keep the bitten limb as still as possible and quietly make your way to the nearest doctor or hospital for an antidote.

Adders react strongly to ground vibrations. If you are walking in adder country, it is sensible to make sure they

Thick-bodied adder, identifiable by the strong diamond pattern (some adders are almost wholly black) and its vertical pupils

feel you coming. You might feel ridiculous stamping along a path through the bracken but you will also know that any adders will quickly get out of the way, if their presence worries you.

In the garden, those with pets might not be too happy to have a resident adder, but on no account should you harm it. If you really don't want it there, call for help from your local herpetological group or the RSPCA for advice. Or make life a bit uncomfortable for it by ensuring there are no nice hiding places, sunning pads or peace and quiet. All a snake really wants from you is no disturbance, somewhere to sunbathe, somewhere to hatch its young, somewhere to hibernate and a place to find what it wants to eat. You'd do better to feel honoured at its presence and take an interest in adders to find out more about them.

First of all, are you sure it's an adder? The identifying mark of the adder is the dark 'diamond' chain along its back but you need to be aware that grass snakes and smooth snakes have separated dark patterns along their backs as well. The grass snake is basically dark green and is easily distinguished by its yellow collar (it is sometimes known as the ringed snake) and by its fondness for water: you often see a grass snake snaking across a pond or river at speed in search of its prey. The markings on a grass snake are more along the side than along the back and are in the form of black bars and spots. Smooth snakes, found mainly in Dorset, are greyish or grey-brown, usually with two rows of darker markings along the back and a heart-shaped marking on top of the head. Their eyes have round pupils, whereas an adder has a vertical pupil set in a reddish iris.

Grass snakes are much the biggest species in Britain: an adder would be lucky to grow to 60cm (2ft) here, but a female grass snake could be as much as twice that size, though the male is more typically less than 90cm (3ft) long;

Grass snake

the average is about 60cm for a male and 75cm (30in) for a female. A big smooth snake might reach about 70cm (27½in). Grass snakes are pathetic, really. They might look quite big but they are defenceless against you. Their first instinct is to scarper, as fast and as noisily as possible. Otherwise they might play dead, lying on their backs with their mouths agape in the hope that you'll just go away and leave them alone, or they might try to scare you off by hissing and pretending to strike, or by writhing about alarmingly and shooting some stinking liquid at you, but the liquid is as harmless as their venomless teeth. Be warned to expect surprises from grass snakes. I once found one,

Smooth snake – rare and harmless, it is not to be confused with the adder. It can be identified by the dark stripe running from its nostrils to neck, broken by the eye

coiled and content, just above head height in a very spiny blackthorn tree.

Smooth snakes are surprisingly docile and they too have no defences: they might bite if really provoked – for example, if you insist on squeezing them – but there is no venom. The smooth snake's diet includes mainly other reptiles (any type of lizard, or the young of other snake species), small mammals (especially 'pinkies') and nestlings, or even slugs, flies and spiders if nothing else is about. Adders eat small mammals (especially and predominantly field voles and mice), nestlings, birds' eggs and also amphibians and lizards; while grass snakes, being semi-aquatic, add fish and amphibians (especially tadpoles) to that menu for preference, along with a few worms and insects – they have also been known on occasion to eat rats as well as voles and mice, though the rats were probably already dead. In their turn, snakes are eaten by various birds of prey, corvids, herons, gulls and even pheasants, and by all sorts of mammalian predators, including foxes, badgers, weasels, hedgehogs, rats and cats.

Please, do learn to love British snakes. You really have nothing to fear from them. It's the foreigners you need to worry about – snakes that have been imported as pets and have escaped. Some of them are harmless, such as the garter snake from North America, but if it doesn't look like a native snake, keep your wits about you and get help from an expert.

Garden Bugs, Slugs and Winged Worriers

Invertebrates: a word to strike a mixture of fear and joy in the hearts of gardeners and householders. This huge group of animals includes anything that doesn't have a backbone. In the context of this book, that means creepy-crawlies and it includes things that fly and swim and slide and scuttle as well as creep and crawl. The biggest invertebrate group in the garden is the arthropods, which all have jointed legs; they include the insects or hexapods (six legs), arachnids (eight legs), chilopods and diplopods (lots and lots of legs), and crustaceans (assorted legs). Other invertebrates are the annelids, with no legs, and the molluscs, which have no legs but one foot! Some of the invertebrates have wings; some have shells; some have feelers; some have pincers; some have stings. Worldwide there are about a million different types of insect alone, and 100,000 species of them are known in Europe. No wonder it's often difficult to tell one bug from another!

If you had the time and skills to count how many invertebrates live in your garden, you would be truly amazed at the variety and the numbers. Spend a lazy hour in the summer lying on the grass and watching: all sorts of intriguing little creatures will parade past you as they go about their daily lives on the ground or on the wing – or under the ground: there are likely to be perhaps 25,000 earthworms in 1,000sq m (1,200sq yd) of soil, and a very important role they are playing there, aerating and draining the soil, recycling vegetable matter, encouraging useful bacteria and giving you manure for free.

Many invertebrates do you similar favours but it is in this huge group of animals that most gardeners also find most of their most infuriating 'pests'. Sometimes the label is unjustified, especially in cases of mistaken identity, and sometimes the animals are indeed causing damage but it is not half as devastating as you might believe. There are many other ways of avoiding problems than by auto-matically killing the animals or by wildly applying chemicals that will eradicate the 'goodies' as well as the 'baddies' and will leave nothing for your garden birds to feed to their nestlings.

Very few of the invertebrates are actually aggressive towards human beings. They are not out to get you, unless they are one of the very tiny group of blood-suckers like horse-flies and mosquitoes looking for a meal. The rest of them will only act against you, if at all, in self-defence, and even then their defences are often pitifully ineffectual against something so huge as a human being. Even those that sting are only doing so because you have threatened them in some way, and for most people (unless you are unlucky enough to be hyperallergic) a sting is no more than an itchy nuisance.

IDENTIKIT

Anybody can recognise a slug or a snail or a ladybird, but can you spot those helpful ladybird larvae, or tell a hover-fly from a wasp, and would you know a lacewing if you saw one? Ladybirds, lacewings and hover-flies are major garden helpers, both as adults and as larvae. And please, please don't regard wasps as pests: they might annoy you for a brief spell in late summer but in fact they, too, are garden helpers.

Sometimes you can say that if it crawls slowly, it is probably a vegetarian and some other animal's prey; it just might be a garden pest, though it might equally be a useful scavenger getting rid of waste matter. You could also say, broadly, that if it moves fast, it is probably a predator and very often the gardener's friend if it is preying on those slow-moving vegetarian pests. But this is by no means a golden rule.

Ants

Here again is an animal that is fascinating to study if only you weren't so intent on stamping on it or throwing boiling water over it. In the garden, ants might steal a few of your smaller seeds, which means that vegetables spring up in unlikely places; they might make nests in the soil or under the lawn or paving, and sometimes unfortunately the nest is under a plant, which will probably wilt. On the plus side, ants also eat small insects that really might be pests, and their nesting labours are good for the texture and drainage of the soil.

Yellow ants are not common in gardens: they are the ones that build big ant heaps in rough grassland. You are more likely to play host to black or red ants. Red ants can sting, but this is no more than an irritation. Black ants are harmless.

Ants can bring great joy to birds, which firstly indulge in the luxury of 'anting' (the birds pick up beakfuls of ants and apply them under their armpits, so to speak, and seem to enjoy doing so) and later to have a glorious feast during the great nuptial flight on a sunny afternoon, when all the flying ants in the neighbourhood seem to swarm within moments of each other. The flying ants won't harm you in any way and the swarm is quickly over. You can easily live with ants in the garden, even though they have this habit of 'milking' aphids for their honeydew. Ants love honeydew, but so do many other insects. Just remember that it's the aphids that produce the stuff, not the ants, and so it is not the ants that are responsible for the fungus that infects uneaten honey-dew deposits and turns the plant leaves black. Mind you, the ants do seem to protect 'their' aphids from predators if they can.

It is only if black ants find their way into the house in response to their sweet tooth that you need to act. Invasions are not at all common and they will probably come in by mistake at first, but if they find a source of sweetness, they'll tell all their friends. Once they have set up a scent trail, the rest will follow it. They won't do any actual harm in the house but you could follow the trail back to the nest, which will probably be within a few strides of the house under the paving or in the lawn. Then, if you really must, you could destroy the nest with boiling water, which is an excessive reaction to such hard-working little creatures. Rather than killing them, or giving them something nasty to take back to the nest, you can take precautions to prevent them from entering in the first place. Check out an organic gardening catalogue (see under 'Useful Information' at the back of this book) for special paints that you can put on thresholds or around pipe holes, or try using mint, cloves or turpentine. Alternatively, try the old trick of drawing a chalk line across their path – oddly, this also sometimes deters cows from going where they are not wanted!

Aphids

Somebody must love aphids – probably their own mothers. It is possible to put in a good word for them, however much you might abhor their appetites and their ability to spread disease from plant to plant. Aphids, bless them, are a major source of meat for a large range of birds and insects. And that honeydew, when it drops to the ground, actually makes a good fertiliser.

An aphid is a true bug, a member of a group that also includes interesting characters like bed bugs and water boatmen and a host of insects that all have a sharp, thin beak used for probing and sucking the juices out of plants or animals. The term 'aphid' covers greenfly, blackfly and whitefly – very tiny insects that make up for their size by their vast numbers. These little things poke those sharp little beaks into their host plants (and they are pretty particular about which plant species they like) to siphon out the sap. From the sap, they absorb protein and as much sugar as they need, squirting out the excess sugar as sticky honeydew.

Aphids reproduce at a prodigious rate, speeding up the process by giving birth to live babies rather than laying eggs, and nearly all the aphids you see for most of the year will be virgin females. A baby aphid, born of a virgin, remains a virgin herself and can give birth to the first of her own clutches of babies when she is only a fortnight old. Actually the life cycle is quite complicated but basically you can blame the girls for damaging your plants. Males, which live for only a few hours, are required to help the colonies survive the winter: they are born from virgin females but in their brief lives their duty is to mate with several females, who will then lay eggs to overwinter and produce the first of the new generations in the following year.

One of the keys to aphid control in the garden is to know on what plants these wintering eggs will be laid. For example, blackfly lay on shrubs such as spindle, philadelphus and guelder rose, which act as hosts for next spring's invasion. Another species, the peach-potato aphid, overwinters its eggs on peach trees but infests potatoes, cabbages and various other plants. Actual cabbage aphids, on the other hand, don't bother with overwintering on a woody host: they lay their eggs on the very brassicas (cultivated or wild relatives) on which they have been feasting all year, so you need to burn old cabbage stalks as soon as you have harvested the crop. Woolly aphids infest and blight apple trees, spending the winter as young, rather than as eggs, in cracks in the bark, where you might see blue tits winkling them out (they look for blackfly eggs, too, in the appropriate shrubs). Greenfly switch from roses in spring to teasels and scabious in summer.

As well as birds, predators of aphids include the adults and larvae of ladybirds, lacewings and hoverflies. Web-spinning spiders also catch large numbers of aphids, even if they are not really interested in eating them.

Bees, wasps and hornets

This group of winged worriers can be well and truly counted among the goodies.

Bees

As well as **honey bees**, there are the big fat **bumble bees** (with several species identifiable by different-coloured bums) that are so often an early sign of spring, and all sorts of **solitary bees** looking for a private little nesting site in your garden and which are a great pleasure to watch as they work. Surely nobody would ever describe any type of bee as a pest – not even the diligent **mason bees** and **mining bees** making their little nests in a wall or creating a very small mound of soil when digging a nest in your lawn, or the **leaf-cutter bee** that carefully cuts out tidy semicircular pieces from rose leaves to make cells for her eggs in her nest burrow in a piece of dead wood somewhere. You might see mason bees working away at soft old mortar but they will hardly bring the house down. All of the mining and mason bees tend to return to their birthplace, which means that over the years they can build up quite a little village of their own.

Nor is there any need to be alarmed by a **swarm**. Genuine swarms will be honey bees whose hive has become too crowded. When this happens, the queen flies out to establish a new colony somewhere else, accompanied by a large number of worker bees that are often so stuffed with honey they would find it quite difficult to sting anything. The swarm will probably settle somewhere while they think about where to go, and then off they rush, following scout bees that have found an ideal new home. If you are alarmed at the sight of a swarm, the bees will ignore you if you don't intrude on them, but contact a local bee keeper if the swarm settles in an inconvenient place. Occasionally they might end up in the loft or even down the chimney, in which case a bit of gentle smoke will persuade them to go somewhere else.

Basically, bees don't use their **stings** to attack but to defend. So a bee won't sting you unless you go and swat it or accidentally trap or nearly squash it, or unless the bees feel that their nest is under threat. It is as well to know where that nest is, because otherwise you might unwittingly put yourself in the way and obstruct the bees' entry to the nest – and that could be considered a threat.

Wasps

The same is true of wasps. You might think that they are deliberately out to attack you, but they are not being aggressive: they are only after something sweet that you are eating or drinking. The more you flap at them, the more they will persist and the more likely you are to be stung (have the antihistamines handy, or use witch hazel). Keep calm and ignore them, or lure them away from you with the goodies they seek: jam, fruit, beer, wine and the like.

Be wary of coming between the wasps and their nests as, like bees, they might think you intend harm to their grubs. And be patient: the 'nuisance' season is very short and only lasts from when the workers have done all their hard work in rearing the grubs and are free for a few weeks from late summer to enjoy themselves by gorging on ripe fruit. As soon as there is a frost, their life is over.

Only a few mated queens survive the winter, tucked away safely in a pile of logs or in an outbuilding or house loft after they have built up their energy reserves browsing on ivy nectar. Keep an eye out for queens looking to hibernate in case they wander in through open upstairs windows by mistake and settle down to overwinter in the folds of your curtains or in hanging clothes (they are attracted to mothballs, by the way). They would be perfectly harmless throughout the winter but it might be wise to

Common wasp

persuade them gently out again before they settle down, so that they can find more suitable quarters elsewhere. In the spring they will emerge and head for the nearest cotoneaster or currant flowers for a feed and then start the labour of nesting, and scraping at the wood on garden sheds and posts to make paper for the nest.

If wasps decide to nest in your loft, it doesn't have to be a problem as long as you just let them get on with their daily lives. The nest is high up and so the wasps will be flying too high to be a 'nuisance'. You might find one or two drifting in through upstairs windows by mistake but they'll soon learn where home is. The nest is a marvellous edifice which you would do well to admire.

Don't kill wasps: they are very useful in the garden. Although the adults like fruit and sweet things, their grubs will be fed on caterpillars, insects and carrion, and a nestful of wasp grubs could chomp its way through literally hundreds of thousands of insects in one summer.

The wasp that bothers you in August is only one of many kinds of garden wasps, some of which are solitary rather than social. Like the bees, they include species that make little nests in walls, dead wood and so on. They also include parasitic wasps, or **ichneumons**, whose 'sting' (if you were molesting the animal) would be no more than a very slight pinprick at most, with no venom – it is actually an ovipostor for laying eggs in caterpillars and other insects. Some of these small dainty wasps are beautiful in close-up and the colours will surprise you. They are sometimes drawn to lighted windows in summer and come indoors but they will do you no harm and you will realise from their persistent buzzing along the inside of a windowpane that they just want to be let out again.

A very large 'wasp' that buzzes past you at speed and sounds like a small helicopter is probably a **hornet** and you

Ichneumon

should count yourself lucky. Hornets are dramatic and quite rare in Britain, found mainly in the south, and I know from experience that you can become quite fond of them. You will usually see them on their own, often flying a regular route as they hunt for insects to feed their young. It is very unusual to be stung by a hornet; they are very laid back and much slower to anger than a wasp, only stinging if they are deliberately attacked. They don't buzz irritatingly around you like wasps, either.

If it is striped with black and yellow, it doesn't necessarily have a sting. The big **horntail**, or giant wood wasp, for example, might look as if it has a sting but the barb is actually for pushing into rotten wood to lay its eggs. Another deceptive stripy family is the **hover-flies** that hang in the air with a faint hum, often quite close to you as you sit in the sun, endlessly patrolling their own patch of sunlight

Hornet

Hover-fly

and darting away suddenly, only to return to exactly the same spot.

These are the animals whose larvae are so useful as aphid eaters, and they are utterly harmless to humans. You can easily recognise hover-flies because they have two wings, whereas wasps and bees have four. They also have larger eyes and smaller antennae than wasps. The adults visit flowers and are good pollinators. To attract hover-flies to your vegetable patch so that they can deal with aphids, plant some marigolds in among the vegetables – any kind will do. If the marigolds happen to be of the African or French type, there is the added bonus that the roots exude something that repels nematodes like potato-root eelworm, as well as depressing the growth of ground elder and couch grass. But don't plant marigolds with cabbages, because the flowers also attract cabbage white butterflies!

Centipedes and millipedes

It is important to differentiate between these two. They are not closely related, despite both being long with a countless number of legs. Both are basically nocturnal and spend the day hidden away under stones or in the soil – anywhere that stays nicely damp.

Centipedes are carnivorous hunters that move fast; they are usually yellow or brown and rather flat in shape. They might look a bit alarming with all those legs and (look closely) what seems to be a pair of pincers at the mouth, but they can't really harm you: at worst, with one of the larger species, they might nip you in self-defence and you might briefly feel a slight stinging sensation.

Millipedes are slow-moving vegetarians and scavengers (they will eat dead slugs and dead worms as well as dead or decaying vegetable matter) and are usually black; they need calcium and so are more common in chalky areas. They are round rather than flat. Millipedes have nothing to bite you with and their means of self-defence is to curl up, or writhe a bit, or to eject a not-so-nice staining fluid if they are frightened. If you find a millipede in a hollowed-out potato, somebody else had already made the first hole before the millipede got to work on it, so don't blame the millipede. One type of millipede, the pill millipede, looks very like a pill woodlouse and they both curl into a ball when alarmed, but the millipede version is shinier and has 34 legs as opposed to the woodlouse's fourteen.

Earwigs

This is another interesting insect, if only you could get all the old wives' tales out of your head. You are very unlikely to find an earwig making for your ear, for a start (unless you happen to sleep on the floor on a straw mattress), and when you learn more about them, they actually become quite endearing. For example, they are wonderful mothers.

Earwigs are nocturnal scavengers and will eat anything, be it plant or animal, live or dead, but the damage they inflict on garden plants is very slight. When an earwig falls out of your prize dahlia or from the crown of an apple you are picking from the tree, it's probably only there as a safe place to be rather than as a source of food, though it does

Earwig

sometimes nibble lightly on flowers and fruit. Give the earwig an alternative home (try the old gardening trick of flower pots stuffed with honey-daubed straw upside down on top of a cane next to the chrysanthemums) and it'll be quite happy to stay there until you release it somewhere else in the morning – preferably by a crevice in bark or some other cranny where it can hide for the rest of the day. Earwigs help you out by eating aphids, moth eggs, small caterpillars, flies and dead insects.

As for those alarming pincers, they are used only in self-defence. They could give you a nip but you'll hardly feel it at all – it'll be no more than a slight sensation of pressure. They won't break your skin or anything as dramatic as that.

Grubs, caterpillars and butterflies

This is where the pest catalogue really begins. Caterpillars hatch from eggs laid by butterflies and moths and, given a chance to munch their way to full size, will in due course go through a pupal or chrysalis stage and eventually emerge as a glorious winged insect to brighten the summer. It seems a great shame to treat them as enemies.

The major offenders in the gardener's eyes are the caterpillars of cabbage white butterflies (large and small), which ravage the leaves of brassicas and nasturtiums. The other butterflies lay their eggs on wild plants. Caterpillars are specialists, and the female butterfly or moth lays her eggs on plants that will feed the caterpillar for the entirety of that stage of its life, so it is worth finding out more about which plants are eaten by which caterpillars. Some of the most attractive butterflies only lay their eggs on stinging nettles.

The moths are more of a problem and the caterpillars of a wide range of moths damage fruit, flowers and vegetables. They include some known misleadingly as worms, such as cutworm (which, some say, can be kept away from tomato plants by driving a large nail into the ground next to the plants). Moths that are a problem indoors are discussed in the next chapter (see pages 196, 198).

Another 'problem' is that some caterpillars are large enough for people to think they might be dangerous and might even be snakes, especially some of the gaudy hawkmoth caterpillars. Caterpillars won't bite or sting and are really not out to hurt you even when they seem to rear up and threaten you; the plump green red-faced caterpillar of the puss moth, for example, is a biggy at about 7cm (2¾in) long and it defies predators by swelling up and lashing about with its two whip-like 'tails' at the rear, but it's all bluster. Never touch a hairy caterpillar, though, as with some species you might well come out in a rash.

Gardeners often come across fat squishy things that are sometimes mistaken for caterpillars but are in fact the larvae of various other insects. Larvae are the young stage of insects after hatching from eggs. If they are the larvae of true flies (*Diptera*) they are legless (though they might have some little prominences that help them to wriggle about) and you might be able to see their biting mouthparts, unless they are typical tapered white-fly maggots with no obvious head but with tiny hooks at the thin end where the head should be. Most larvae of Hymenoptera (ants, wasps, bees and the like) are also legless as they are usually surrounded by their food and don't need to go anywhere. Moth and butterfly caterpillars always have legs, and the larvae of sawflies are also legged and look very like caterpillars. Beetle larvae have six legs, if you look closely. Do not assume that all larvae are bad guys: it is important to be able to distinguish the good ones, like the aphid-hunting larvae of ladybirds, lacewings and hover-flies.

Some 'good' larvae

Lacewing larvae are shaped like skittles, tapered at both ends, with little clusters of bristles on each segment and six legs; they have a pair of 'fangs' or pincers at the front and are usually greenish, brownish or dirty white but sometimes they camouflage themselves with the empty skins of their victims (which include spider mites as well as aphids). Eggs hang under leaves from slender gum threads. A single adult lacewing could eat as many as a thousand aphids in two months.

Lacewing larva

Ladybird larvae might remind you of tiny crocociles. They are slate-grey, usually with small patches of colour (red or yellow, depending on the species) and have six legs; they also have those little clusters of bristles on each segment. A ladybird larva will munch a few hundred aphids within the three weeks or so before it becomes a pupa that looks very like a bird-dropping. Ladybird eggs are yellow and skittle-shaped, laid in batches on aphid-infested plants.

Ladybird larva

Hover-fly larvae are flattened and pale green or fawn; being true flies, the larvae are legless. The pupae are pear-shaped and are found on leaves near aphid colonies.

Hover-fly larva

Ground beetle larvae are rather like elongated beetles: you can see the six legs, the pincer-like mouthparts and a pincer-like pair at the back end as well. The dark body is a series of segments with a slight indentation forming a line down the middle.

Ground beetle larva

Some 'bad' larvae

Leatherjackets are plump, dull greyish-brown grubs that will eventually become daddy-longlegs or crane-flies. They chomp their way through the roots of lawn grasses and various other plants. At the front end there is a rather odd flat, star-shaped 'face'. Adults sometimes come into the house, batting about the room if the lights are on; they like a drop of nectar but don't feed much in their short lives.

Leatherjacket

Cockchafer (maybug) larvae are fat, white, curved, caterpillar-like grubs with brown to reddish heads, tiny reddish spots in a row down the sides and six legs. Cockchafer grubs are destructive root-eaters, especially in grassland and lawns, where each grub lives for several years. The big chestnut-coloured adult beetles (maybugs) strip the leaves from a wide range of trees, as well as crashing against your lighted windows on May evenings, sounding hard enough almost to break the glass. If the adults do come into the room, they career around like flying drunks.

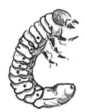 

Cockchafer larva and adult maybug

Stag beetle larvae look very similar to cockchafer grubs but live on rotting wood in old tree stumps; the adults do no harm at all, except in fighting each other, which is what they use their 'antlers' for. Stag beetles are endangered, so please don't confuse the grubs with cockchafers! If it's a fat white thing in dead wood, it's very different from a fat white thing under the grass.

Stag beetle larva

Wireworms are not good news in the garden. These are the yellowish grubs of click beetles and live in the ground for several years, chomping the roots of a wide range of plants and tunnelling into runner-bean seeds before they have a chance to germinate. They are especially a problem on newly cultivated grassland – for example, if you decide to dig up a bit of the lawn and turn it into a carrot bed. The larvae look rather like tough worms but with six short legs at the front and a small pair of 'pincers' at the back. The adult beetles are dirty brown and have the ability to flip over in a dramatic series of high somersaults and with a loud click if they find themselves on their back. Amazing.

Wireworm, or click beetle grub

Horse-flies

As with mosquitoes, it is only female horse-flies that go for blood; the males sup nectar. Horse-flies are daytime flyers and unbelievably persistent once they have located a large mammal host, including humans. Really the only answer is to swat them or go indoors. Some of them warn of their approach but others, known as cleg-flies, sneak up silently, landing with a silent thud, and are especially annoying when the weather is thundery. Their bites can swell up and itch like crazy. If you get a chance to look a horse-fly in the eye, you might be surprised at the colour and patterns you see there.

Midges, gnats and mozzies

This collection of very small flies often cause annoyance, even when they don't bite. It's something about that very high whine, perhaps, that some of them make – you tend to associate the whine with an imminent bite and all the itching that such bites produce. Well, not all whiners are human blood-suckers.

The group includes those clouds of winter gnats that seem to be attracted to something prominent but don't bite; their larvae feed on rotting leaves. There are also clouds of non-biting midges, which lay their eggs in water; their larvae are the 'bloodworms' you might find in the garden pond or the rainwater butt. Other midges get into your hair on summer evenings and make you scratch furiously but don't bring you out in bumps in the way that biting mosquitoes do. The latter only bite you if they are females (the males are wimpish and only feed on nectar, not blood); they breed in water, as do the more common mosquitoes that come into the bedroom by mistake and send you diving for cover, though they are actually in search of bird blood, not human blood, so you can relax.

If biting mosquitoes are really a problem, you need to dry up: if they have no stagnant water in which to lay their eggs, they'll go somewhere else.

More bugs and beetles

True bugs are distinguished from beetles by their juice-sucking proboscis, rather than a beetle's biting mouthparts, and also by the way their front wings usually overlap halfway, whereas a beetle's wings generally lie alongside each other. Aphids, for example, are bugs but maybugs are beetles.

Some of the beetles are dark nocturnal ground hunters doing good work on your behalf by predating slugs and maggots, but also perhaps enjoying your fruit. Ground beetles include the very black **devil's coach-horse**, which rather alarmingly turns to face you if it thinks you are on the attack and then arches up its back end like a scorpion, opens its big jaws and simultaneously expels something very smelly from its abdomen. It could even nip you but this won't do any damage and it's only in self-defence. Let it be: it is trying to rid your garden of slugs and various harmful grubs.

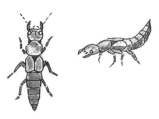

Devil's coach-horse

Flea beetles are so named because they jump. They can be pests on particular plants, such as potatoes, or turnips and other brassicas. You can tell that a flea beetle has been at work on the brassicas when you see tidy round holes in the leaves of seedlings. The beetles are very tiny and the turnip flea is brightly patterned with yellow stripes. Larvae go for the roots.

Weevils, characterised by their long snouts, are also beetles and include the destructive pea weevil, apple blossom weevil, grain weevil (an indoor pest) and pine weevil (bane of the forester). There are some very pretty weevils about, in a range of splendid colours.

Slugs and snails

Pests? Oh yes they are! Well, some of them are. Some are carnivores but most are not fussy about what they eat and go for rotting vegetable matter, fungi and even carrion. A cheeky few prefer green, growing plants and these are the ones that cause problems in the garden. Those yellow slugs really only eat rotten vegetation and moulds and you tend to find them in or near the house. The big black ones actually prefer rotting stuff but will go for greens if they can't find some decaying plant matter. (Don't be fooled by a slug's named colour: they often have different colours within the same species and the big black ones might also be reddish-orange or yellowish.) The smaller ones – the netted slug and the garden slug – are the real culprits.

Snails are probably worse than slugs, in that they climb up the plants. Among them, the common or garden snail is a major plant gobbler but it is pollution-conscious and doesn't like living near industrial smoke. Some people used to eat garden snails, though the more commonly eaten species is the larger Roman snail of England's southern chalklands. If you do decide that eating garden snails is the best way of reducing their population, don't eat them straight out of the garden, as they will taste of what they've been eating. Feed them for a few days on something clean, like washed lettuce.

Slugs and snails are largely creatures of the night, taking cover during the day but often coming out after a shower. They are quite fussy: they like damp conditions, though not too much rain for a slug; but they don't like a dry night either, as they quickly become desiccated. They have eyes, but these can really only tell the difference between light and dark, and you can sometimes lure them at night with a dim light.

Favourite hiding places for snails include flower pots: you often find almost completely encrusted pots in a sheltered, shady spot, especially in winter or when they aestivate (close down in a dry summer). A pile of stones or logs will do nicely too. Slugs sometimes hide between or under paving stones, or under loose bark, and will also burrow into the soil when there is a danger of drying out too much. A dry atmosphere is the greatest enemy to slugs and snails and they protect their soft bodies with mucus, which also helps them to slide along the ground.

Woodlice

In one of my old homes, the stone floors were carpeted with woodlice: you had to watch where you walked or there would be that pathetic little crunching sound as you trod on one by mistake. Woodlice are terrestrial crustaceans, related to the crustaceans of the seas such as crabs, lobsters, barnacles and shrimps. With such connections, woodlice still need a damp habitat and quickly lose body moisture in a dry atmosphere.

There are several species, ranging from brown to grey or black, and they are scavengers living among decaying vegetation. They don't do much harm to living plants: they usually chew up dead leaves and other dead or dying plant parts, or graze on algae, or find something to eat in dung, but they do sometimes taste your seedlings and even graze your lawn lightly. Like millipedes and centipedes, they don't like the light and you usually find them hiding under stones, logs and plant pots. Another likeness with millipedes is that woodlice can excrete a repellent fluid if threatened but can do no harm at all to human beings.

They have seven pairs of legs and the back five pairs are used for breathing: they need to be covered with a film of water, because they act like the gills of a fish. The crunchy covering that protects their bodies needs calcium and that is why you often find woodlice at the base of a wall – mortar between stones and bricks is based on lime. They are truly intriguing animals that are worth getting to know: much about their lifestyle will surprise you.

The main predators on woodlice are shrews, toads, centipedes, ground beetles, harvestmen, wolf spiders and a chestnut-coloured night-hunting spider (*Dysdera* species) that specialises in attacking woodlice. They are also attacked by certain parasites and of course by humans who mistakenly believe that they are harmful. Apart from those little nibbles in seedlings, they don't do any harm in the garden or the house, so don't persecute them. Just because you happen to find a woodlouse hiding under a damaged plant, don't automatically blame it for the damage – it is probably innocent.

Worms

Earthworms are definitely not pests. They are the very foundation of a good garden. Some gardeners get worked up about worm casts on the lawn but if you let these dry and then brush them about, they make excellent manure for the grass.

Strangely, the front end of an earthworm is the sharp end, not the blunt one. Worms basically want to be hidden: their instinct is to get away from light as quickly as possible and burrow back to safety in the soil. As they are prey to many birds, hedgehogs, shrews, moles, amphibians, reptiles and some of the bigger carnivores, it is hardly surprising that they feel safer below ground. They tend to migrate to the surface at night to feed, and then make their way down again before dawn. They are vegetarians but only eat *dead* plant matter, which they suck into their bodies and eventually excrete as manure. They also tend to pull dead leaves down into their burrows to eat, but are just as likely to forget about them and leave them to break down, releasing nutrients into the soil. Only a couple of species excrete their casts above ground.

DEALING WITH IT

If you do think you have a pest problem in the garden and you can identify what is causing it, you can plan your campaign – and really the campaign should begin before the pest has even thought of becoming a problem.

Natural predators

The most useful tip is to encourage natural predators to do the job for you. That means toads, frogs and hedgehogs for a start. Hedgehogs eat a wide range of invertebrates, including beetles, caterpillars, centipedes, harvestmen, spiders, flies and slugs. Foxes can help too: I know of a Yorkshire vet who takes great pride in his garden and regularly patrols it by torchlight at night to collect snails. He takes the snails down to his local wildlife rescue centre and they are fed to the foxes! Foxes and badgers will dig out nuisances like the cockchafer grubs and leatherjackets that are ruining your lawn, though of course the mammals do their own type of harm during the digging. If you haven't got foxes, run some free-range chickens and ducks around the place; ducks, in particular, are great slug gobblers. So are shrews and, above all, slow-worms.

The wild bird population which you have been encouraging in the garden will play a major role in keeping pest invertebrates from running riot. Song thrushes are the great experts with snails, and blackbirds and missel thrushes eat them too. Slugs, poor souls, have no hard shell to protect them and they are eaten by the same birds (and sometimes by pheasants). They are even eaten by some of the larger beetles, and I have watched the flat, anonymous-looking larva of a glow-worm slowly but relentlessly chomping its way through a large, living snail.

There are plenty of 'good' bugs in the garden that will act as natural predators of the 'bad' bugs. Centipedes are fast-moving, many-legged hunters that eat many types of soil pest. Ground beetles go for slugs and the grubs of cabbage root fly – make them feel welcome by providing flat stones or pieces of wood under which they can shelter. The alarming-looking devil's coach horse is bad news for slugs and larvae. Spiders, of course, catch all sorts of flying insects in their webs, or hunt for insects on the ground or in plants. Lacewings, ladybirds and hoverflies are the great aphid hunters.

Wise planting

Predators apart, you can take steps to ensure that your plants can fight back. If you grow healthy plants in the first place, they are much more able to resist any attacks. If you rotate your 'crops' (including flowers), you will be able to avoid pest build-ups, and if you mix up your plantings rather than growing large patches or rows of one thing, you will confuse a pest that likes a particular group of plant species.

Organic gardening

Get yourself a really good guide to organic gardening and follow its advice. One of the first things it will tell you is that pesticides (whether they are aimed at insects, weeds or fungi) can damage not only non-target species but your own health as well as that of the target. Another thing you will learn is that there are better ways of encouraging healthy plant growth than by using chemical fertilisers. Above all, organic gardeners respect their environment and work with it rather than against it, seeking to preserve the balance of nature, and in doing so they use up-to-date scientific techniques as well as sound traditional practices. They concentrate on prevention: growing the right plant in the right place at the right time, growing plants that are naturally resistant to whatever your local problem might be, rotating plant types to avoid pest build-up, avoiding monoculture, encouraging natural predators, and employing physical rather than chemical barriers against pests.

Physical methods

Think very carefully before blasting 'pests' with garden poisons. Think about physical methods first: removing pests by hand, for example, or setting a trap specifically for that type of pest. Hunt down adults before they propagate a new generation: it is much easier to deal with one adult maybug or cranefly than all its offspring. Above all, think about keeping them out in the first place. Here are some ways of guarding against pests and keeping them away from the plants before they lay their eggs.

Companion planting

Companion planting means growing certain plants close to certain other plants to the benefit of both. There are several aspects to companion planting. Firstly, growing certain plants with others often helps each plant to thrive. Secondly, mixing plants in this way fools pests, especially if you are growing strong-smelling plants among your vegetables. Thirdly, and again to confuse pests, mixing different sorts of plants together makes the pest's target far more elusive. Try some of the following mixtures:

- Marigolds with tomatoes or potatoes
- Chives with carrots
- Borage with strawberries
- Celery with leeks
- Cucumbers with broccoli
- Gooseberries with tomatoes
- Chamomile with just about anything
- Nettles near tomatoes and near aromatic herbs
- Beans and carrots and cauliflower and potatoes
- Carrots and lettuces and peas or onions
- Turnips, carrots and radishes near peas and beans
- Parsley near roses to keep greenfly away

Mixtures to avoid:

- Cabbages and strawberries
- Fennel near anything
- Gladioli near beans
- Onions or garlic with peas or beans
- Potatoes close to apple trees
- Sage with cucumber
- Spindleberry or philadelphus (major overwintering for blackfly) near broad beans

Flying pests

- Drape finely spun nylon 'cobwebs' or fine mesh over the plants.
- Make a vertical barrier of fine mesh or polythene, about 60cm (2ft) high, around carrots: carrot flies will not fly higher than this, and the barrier also provides a good microclimate for the carrots.
- Grow vulnerable plants under polytunnels or in cold frames.
- Put collars of tarred paper or roofing felt around cabbage plants to deter cabbage root flies.
- Spread some grass mowings lightly over brassica plants to deter cabbage white butterflies from laying their eggs on the leaves.

Crawling pests

- Put small squares of carpet underfelt around each plant to deter cabbage root fly.
- Put an inverted yoghurt pot with a hole punched into the base for the plant to grow through, to keep out other root flies, cutworms and cabbage moths.
- Grow each plant surrounded by its personal little greenhouse made from cut-down plastic bottles (keeps the slugs away until the plant is big enough to fend for itself, and helps the plant to grow well in a microclimate).

Caterpillars

With damaging caterpillars, the trick is to recognise the eggs before they even become caterpillars. Use a good guide to make sure that the eggs are from a pest. You will usually find eggs on the underside of the host plant's leaves and quite often you can spot the butterfly or moth in the very act of laying them. Wipe off the eggs and destroy them. If they have already hatched, pick off the caterpillars while they are still small and, ideally, put them somewhere else to feed birds and wasps. For those who are not squeamish, caterpillars can be squished in your fingers but don't touch a hairy caterpillar with bare hands.

Slugs and snails

Slugs are most people's bugbear and many ingenious physical tricks have been used by those who are aware that slug pellets can damage a lot more than slugs. The first thing to remember is that slugs come out at night but hide away during the day. Give them somewhere to hide where you can find them and remove them, or go out at night to look for them when they are active (the term is relative).

- Something gritty sprinkled around plants will fend off slugs and snails – crushed eggshells, dry cinders, shredded bark, dry soot, or products you can find in organic gardening catalogues.
- Uses a very low electric fence (tricky, this one) against slugs.
- Slugs hate copper. Use self-adhesive copper tape around plant pots and tubs, or stand them on commercial copper-containing mats.
- Get some ducks – they are great ones for eating slugs.
- Go out at night (especially in damp weather) and spot your slugs by torchlight. Gather them up (use an implement of some kind to avoid getting slimy fingers) and feed them to the ducks, transport them to a grassy roadside verge or, more wastefully, pop them into salty water.
- The good old beer trap: put some weak beer into a shallow container and sink in it into the soil at ground level (add some brown sugar to increase the attraction). The slug drops in for a pint and in theory drowns

happy. But other more desirable small things might drop in as well, in which case you should raise the level of the rim of the container. There are more sophisticated slug traps on the market in various organic gardening catalogues.

- Put an encouraging layer of something on the ground – old carpet, damp newspaper, planks, large flower pots, or cabbage leaves: the slugs (and probably earwigs and woodlice) will take cover underneath during the day and you can collect them and dispose of them. But where? Surely you wouldn't toss them into your neighbour's garden, would you? If you do, the joke's on you: the slugs will find their way 'home' again. Take them further away and find them such a nice habitat that they won't want to come back.

- Lure slugs to the daytime doss-house with the irresistible scent of goodies: orange peel, apples, ripe bones, over-ripe grapes, rotting carrots. Better still, combine the lure with the shelter: dripping smeared on lettuce leaves, or cabbage leaves that have been slightly steamed to soften them and then rubbed with butter or dripping, or melon rind, empty grapefruit halves, rhubarb leaves, damp rotted straw, a damp plastic bag (fill it with something green), a beer-and-flour paste spread on the underside of a flat piece of wood.

With snails, some of the same tricks can be used but also try the following:

- Encourage thrushes, the main devourer of snails, and give them access to stone anvils on which to smash their prey.
- Make sure your garden soil is not alkaline: snails need calcium for shell-building.

- Sprinkle a barrier of sharp sand around your plants, or put down coarse sandpaper.
- If the plants can stand it, sprinkle a barrier of salt thinly on the outer edge of your sand carpet.
- Use bran as a lure before a snail hunt.
- Give up growing plants that your snails have become addicted to.

The old-fashioned ways

The Sussex agricultural and horticultural publisher J Baxter, in the early nineteenth century, was all for striking a balance with nature. Discussing the 'almost numberless' insects that infested grain, seeds and young plants, he was 'rather inclined (convinced of the utter impossibility of total extermination when having once made an attack) to recommend the old adage "live and let live"; for, as an intelligent contributor to this work very justly observes, "insects will come, they will eat and must be fed": this gentleman, aware of the folly of counteracting nature, sows a double quantity of seed, and thus insures a crop.'

Baxter also knew all about prevention: 'In order to prevent the introduction of insects into gardens, plantations, &c., the only means are good culture, and a judicious choice of soil and situation; if the above circumstances are attended to, it is seldom that insects will prevail to any injurious extent. But when such are beyond our control, as they frequently are, the only alternative is to prevent their ravages, either by their utter removal by hand, or by means of some kind of application.' Some of his ideas are mentioned in the boxed text 'Some general hints', mingled with other old methods of dealing with insect pests.

Some general hints

- Bring in ducks for slugs, but chickens around fruit trees to gobble up codling moths and other pests.
- Hand-pick insect pests whenever you can; if they are in trees, try shaking them down into sheets, and then drown, crush or burn them. Caterpillars are sometimes attracted to pieces of rag hung in the trees.
- Pepper was an old standby: finely ground pepper against slugs, or a mixture of oatmeal, coarse sugar and ground pepper against ants, woodlice and beetles. Salt was scattered as a slug and snail barrier.
- Boiling water is vicious but quick. Old gardeners would pour it straight on to slugs, woodlice, ants and other poor creatures. They also poured it around the stems or roots of trees if there was an aphid problem, but the reasoning eludes me.

Ants

In theory, ants will not cross a line drawn with chalk. More realistically, if ants are coming into the greenhouse, put a line of fruit-tree banding grease, about 2.5cm (1in) wide, across their regular route. Ants can also be repelled with mint, cloves or turpentine. They will be attracted to a nice piece of crispy bacon laid on the ground: they will collect underneath it and you can then dunk the bacon, ants and all, in water (if you must – what harm have ants ever done to you?).

Aphids and mites

- To deter **blackfly**, pinch out the growing tips of **broad bean** plants as soon as three rings of pods are well established; or plant broad beans in November. If the blackfly is already on the plant, use a solution of 115g (4oz) soft soap, not detergent, dissolved in 11 litres (2½ gallons) of water.
- For **greenfly**, encourage ladybirds, lacewings and hoverflies: their larvae will devour greenfly by the million. Make sure you can identify those larvae. Or try a spray made by simmering onions in water, mashed, strained and cooled. Or add the strained water from boiling up rhubarb leaves in a soapy solution as for blackfly. Or use a wash of soot water.
- Use a **seaweed derivative** as an **aphid** deterrent, applied weekly; it is also a foliar feed for the plants.
- Grow **African marigolds** next to vulnerable greenhouse plants to protect them from **whitefly**.
- Smoke a cigarette in the greenhouse! In the old days, gardeners would fumigate red mite and other nuisances with **tobacco smoke. Henbane** was also used, as a spray.

Biters

While you are hanging around a stable, you might want to protect yourself from biting insects (horse-flies, midges and mosquitoes). You could always make up your own repellent. The old recipe for Dover's Pomade was 14g (½oz) of oil of citronella, 7g (¼oz) of oil of cedarwood and 14g (½oz) of spirit of camphor. Alternatively, rub your bare skin with mint. If you do get bitten by a horse-fly, quickly apply a paste made from bicarbonate of soda and water if you don't have any antihistamines handy.

Carrot fly

Thin ribbons of material soaked in paraffin and laid beside rows of young carrots should deter carrot fly, as will all sorts of other powerful smells. The paraffin won't affect the crop itself – the fumes will long since have evaporated by the time the carrots are ready for harvesting. Don't sow your carrots too thickly: the smell of bruised carrot foliage when you thin them out will surely bring the fly at the double. Choose a showery day for thinning.

Caterpillars

- For **gooseberry caterpillars**, invite **cuckoos** into your garden.
- As a spray against assorted caterpillars, steep **elder flowers** in boiling water, strain and cool.
- When planting out **cabbages**, put half a crushed mothball or some pieces of rhubarb into the planting hole first, to prevent club root.
- Grow **lavender** around the vegetable patch if large white butterflies are a problem on **brassicas**. (The drawback to this old remedy is that large whites love lavender, so although they will happily flock around it and in theory ignore the cabbages, in practice it might also attract them to that part of the garden.)

Cockchafer grubs

For cockchafer grubs, hand-picking was the rule in the days when farm labour was cheap: men, women and children followed the plough, picked up the grubs, popped them into baskets and then simply chucked them into the nearest ditch – the animals would not be able to burrow back into the soil and would soon be picked up by predators or die of exposure. Another method was to plough the area and then put in plenty of ducks or other poultry to gobble up the grubs. Pigs also relished them. Above all you encouraged rooks, because they just loved these fat white grubs. If you had horses, apparently 'stable urine' was just the thing (full of ammonia): you watered the infested ground with it to knock out cockchafer grubs and leatherjackets. Stable urine was also poured around the roots of gooseberry bushes and apple trees in winter to kill off gooseberry caterpillars and apple blighters.

Wireworm

If wireworms are a problem, slice up some potatoes or carrots and place the slices on the ground. Examine them daily. The wireworms will congregate on them in large numbers and you can then gather up the hordes and dispose of them in one way or another – boiling water is instant.

Some modern ways

Organic gardening catalogues are full of new ideas using the latest technology, much of it based on using natural predators or parasites. Some of the interesting products on the market, obtainable either by mail order or from good garden centres, include:

- Barrier glue to deter vine weevils, winter moths, ants and earwigs
- Fleece tunnels and blankets to protect crops from flying pests
- Sticky traps for whitefly and other greenhouse pests
- Screens to keep small flying insects out of the greenhouse
- Safe natural sprays for aphids and red spider mite that won't harm beneficial insects
- Ready-made soft-soap solution as a spray against aphids and red spider mite

- Pheromone-based moth traps (species-specific sex pheromones lure them to a sticky end)
- Insect-repellent sprays and candles
- Nonpoisonous selective insecticides
- Slug granules – physical barrier combined with slime-sucker
- Plant-based snail repellents
- Cockroach and woodlice traps
- Parasites that specifically kill slugs, or vine weevils, or leatherjackets (daddy-longlegs grubs in the lawn – a favourite of badgers and birds), or cockchafer grubs (those fat white ones with orange-red heads that eat grass roots and turn your grass yellow – if it hasn't already been torn out by foxes, rooks and starlings hunting for the grubs)
- Ladybird larvae and lacewing larvae to eat your aphids
- Mites that eat other mites and thrips
- Bugs that eat mealy bugs
- Parasites that eliminate whitefly
- Bee kits to encourage pollinators

The list of natural 'bio' predators is endless and there's a whole new gardening world out there!

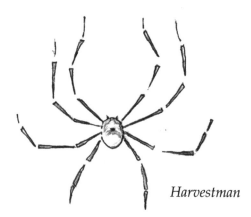

Harvestman

| Bugs Indoors |

Invertebrates indoors can be just a bit of a nuisance, like flying insects buzzing around or beating against the light bulbs and windows, or can be illogically frightening, like spiders. They can be blood-suckers, like fleas and ticks; or, in some cases, can spell serious trouble when they attack the very fabric of the house. Many of them are unseen, or only come out at night.

NO WINGS

Many legs

These include woodlice, millipedes and centipedes, which do find their way into houses but are not really a problem. Woodlice and millipedes, as explained on pages 161–2, need dampness to survive. They eat rotting vegetation, which might include rotting wood indoors, but they are not responsible for starting the rot. There is a long-legged centipede that quite often lives on house walls and moves at a mighty lick, but it is perfectly harmless to homes and humans.

Eight legs

The eight-leggers are not insects: they are arachnids and the group includes spiders, mites, ticks, harvestmen and scorpions. None of the arachnids have wings. There are no native scorpions in Britain, but there is something called a false scorpion – so tiny that you are unlikely to notice it, though some species are predators on booklice. Ticks are outdoor animals, though you or your pets might bring one inside by mistake when it latches on for a blood meal – a meal which, you might be relieved to know, can last that tick for many, many months. It is a bad mistake to try to yank off a tick, as you will simply leave the mouthparts embedded in the flesh and this could lead to infection. Instead, you need to persuade it to let go and drop off (which it would do anyway once it has had its fill). A dab of methylated spirits is one traditional method, as is, with great care, a quick singe with a lighted cigarette.

Harvestmen

Harvestmen are not quite spiders. They are the ones with a small body in the middle of a set of eight very long and spindly legs. They don't spin webs; they don't have any venom; they have only two eyes (most spiders have eight); their body is unipart (spiders' bodies are in two parts); and they are mainly nocturnal. They prey on all sorts of living or dead small creatures such as spiders, centipedes and caterpillars; they also eat carrion and fungi. You are most likely to notice them in late summer, hence their name: this is when they usually mature. There are many different species and you might find them resting on house walls or outside on tree trunks during the day. Some of the shorter-legged species tend to live on the ground. None of them do any harm at all to people or their homes but if they give you the creeps, catch them up gently, as described for house spiders, taking extra care not to damage their very fragile legs.

Mites

Mites include a wide range of species, all of them measured in mere millimetres, with a wide range of habits. Many of them are outdoor animals, like the tiny and carnivorous red velvet mite you sometimes see on a garden path in spring, or the even tinier but pestilential red spider mite that infests fruit trees and greenhouse plants (and, sometimes, house plants). Indoors, the problem mites are ones that infest cereals, flour or dried fruit, and also the dust mite that causes problems for those with allergies. Most of the indoor mites like slightly damp conditions and dislike central heating. Another possible house visitor is the clover mite, which you might see swarming up the walls like a rusty patch in motion; the mites are searching for egg-laying sites and would much prefer to find crevices in bark. They won't do any actual harm indoors.

Spiders

Quite a few people will admit to shuddering at the sight of a spider, and many more find it difficult to pick one up. Silly, really – none of the native spiders in Britain can hurt you. Even the very, very few that would bite in self-defence if you handled them roughly would find it difficult to pierce your skin and even if they succeeded, their venom would do no more than give mild irritation. They have no desire to taste human flesh anyway.

Spiders are amazing creatures and well worth getting to know. If you do have a bit of a phobia about spiders indoors, find out all you can about them and the fear will gradually vanish. Don't be put off by the fact that most spiders have eight eyes; just admire the fact that they can all make silk, even if they don't all use it to spin webs.

You can take a rough guess at the type of spider by its web, even without seeing the spinner. The typical big hairy house spider makes a slapdash cobweb that anybody can recognise. The garden spider, recognisable by the white cross on its abdomen, is one of the orb-web spiders that make those beautiful cartwheel webs (you might find the web of the closely related zygiella spider on your window frames). A large number of species in the linyphiid group make the hammocks or sheets that sometimes cover the grass (money spiders make a smaller version), while another group, the theridiids, make scaffold webs, with horizontal and vertical threads interlocking. My cottage is often home to the daddy-longlegs spider – with very long, almost invisibly thin legs and a small body (quite hard to see the spider at all sometimes) – which makes a rather flimsy web near the ceiling and reacts to your touch on the web by vibrating it crazily so that the spider itself bounces up and down at a dizzying rate on its own trampoline. Otherwise these spiders rarely move from their webs.

All spiders are predators but not all spiders set silken traps for their prey. Some lie in ambush and spring out to catch whatever is passing; others actively hunt their prey and you can see them on the run – or even on the jump, like my all-time garden favourite, the compact, sharp-eyed little zebra spider, which hunts by sight on my sunny doorstep and garden path or up the warm brick wall and can jump at least 10cm (4in) almost on command. Crab spiders in the garden usually loiter in flowers, often of matching colour for better camouflage; they are so named because they walk sideways like a crab.

All spiders kill their prey with a stab of the fangs aimed at the back of the victim's head and quickly paralysing it with venom. Spiders don't have teeth to chew their food: they suck the juices from the victim's body instead. Female house spiders are capable of going for several months without eating or drinking anything at all; they are the ones that take up residence in your home and make those dusty triangular corner cobwebs, while the smaller males are the ones that come running into the house in the autumn in search of the females, always moving at speed and quite offended when you pop them back outside.

Don't, please don't, kill your house spiders, even the ones in the bath. If you can't bear to pick them up gently in your bare hands and put them in a friendly shed, use a clear plastic tub (the sort that you sometimes get in supermarkets) and place it carefully over the spider, doing this slowly so that it doesn't bolt, and slide a piece of stiff card underneath to shut the door. Then it is quite easy to take it outside. A light plastic container is much kinder than a glass, which could easily crush a stray leg. Alternatively, gently drop a handkerchief over it, but then you can't see what's happening underneath.

As for house spiders in the bath and the eternal mystery of how they got there, they are more likely to have fallen in by mistake from the edge of the bath or the wall than to have climbed up the wastepipe – you'll still find the occasional spider in the bath even if you keep the plug in and block the overflow. They really don't want to be there at all, so rescue them.

Cottagers used to swear that conkers placed on the floor near the wainscot would keep spiders away. More realistically, if there are no insects in your house as prey for spiders, there should be no spiders.

Six legs

... And several tails

There is a very primitive group of insects that include the bristletails and the springtails. Among them are two indoor types: silverfish and firebrats.

Silverfish move very quickly, like slivers of mercury: they are small, about 1cm (less than ½in) long and silvery white, with flat elongated tapered bodies, long antennae at the front and three long 'tails' at the other end. They are nocturnal and you are most likely to see them rushing out of sight when you open a kitchen cupboard or drawer. They like moist conditions and eat starchy things like paper (including wallpaper and its paste), bookbindings, old photographs, watercolour paintings and flour, and prefer a moist atmosphere. Thus the first protective action you can take is to air and dry the kitchen (or possibly bathroom) that they are infesting. Fill in any floor or skirting-board cracks where they might hide.

Silverfish

Firebrats are more likely to be a problem in a bakery than a home and are also found in heating ducts. They are very like silverfish but are brown and more bristly.

... And itchy

Lice are wingless parasites on mammals (including humans) and birds. They have flattened round or oval bodies; some species have biting jaws and mainly go for birds, while others have sucking mouthparts to draw the blood out of mammals and one of these specifically chooses human blood.

Fleas are also wingless but their bristled bodies are flattened from side to side and of course they famously leap. Most are brown or black and all of them are blood-suckers. In the home, you might find dog fleas, cat fleas, rabbit fleas or human fleas – and cat fleas are just as happy to launch themselves on to humans. Watch out for their pearly white eggs and slim white larvae in your dog's or cat's bed. If your dog lives outside in a kennel, the old country trick was to grow fennel nearby to deter fleas.

... And chirrupy

You don't see them so often now in the home, but the cricket on the hearth used to become quite a pet in some old cottages. Crickets are closely related to locusts and also to grasshoppers, which also come indoors in the summer, quite by mistake – you might find them on the ceiling and they jump a mile if you put a finger near them.

Bush-crickets are outdoor types, though one or two are attracted to lights at night. The so-called true crickets include the field cricket, the wood cricket and the house cricket. The last of these is said to warble like a bird: it chirps at the rate of two or three per second, and continues on and on and on and on . . . lovely when you first hear it but the endless repetition all night long can become irritating. Otherwise, house crickets are harmless.

FLYERS

Flies

The family of 'true' flies is huge, with more than 5,000 species in Britain. Most of them are day animals and all of

them live on liquid meals that range from nectar to blood or
dung juices. All of them have legless larvae, some of which
spend their larval stage under water, others on land and
some as parasites. The flies that come into the house include
buzzers such as house-flies, bluebottles and cluster-flies;
they also include thunderflies, which are not true flies.

Bluebottles

Bluebottles are big, stout blow-flies. The females are
irresistibly drawn to the smell of meat and fish in the house
– the perfect home for laying their eggs, so that the fat white
larvae can have a feast on slightly rotting flesh. A dustbin is
a joy to bluebottles and, as your mother will have told you,
you just don't know where they've been. Their Latin name,
disgustingly, is *Calliphora vomitoria*, which speaks volumes.
If bluebottles or house-flies are a problem, always make
sure that all food is covered so that they cannot get
anywhere near it, and wrap your rubbish in newspaper
even when it is in the bin.

Cluster-flies

Cluster-flies are also blow-flies but they lay their eggs on
earthworms, which the larvae eat alive. The adults come
into houses to hibernate in large groups in attics, on curtains
and in sheds; they are rather dopey and drab flies but if you
look closely, you will find that they have golden hairs on the
thorax (the body section where the wings sprout from) and
a chequered pattern on the abdomen.

House-flies

House-flies are smaller than the blow-flies and they like to
breed in dung or something that is decaying. There are
many different species but all you really need to know is
that they can carry disease and they leave nasty specks of

vomit and droppings on both horizontal and vertical surfaces. Like blow-flies, house-flies 'eat' by sopping up liquids, and they spread disease by regurgitating over your food after they've been having a sup on carrion or dung. Clean up all those little black and brown spots of fly vomit and excreta immediately.

Flimsy flyers

Some delicate flying insects sometimes come indoors, either attracted to the lights or to hibernate. Their flight is rather weak, as if they don't really mean to be flying at all, and they tend to have long, fragile-looking antennae. They include the gentle lacewing, whose larvae are described on page 165, with its slender green or light-brown body and long transparent wings held along the body. If you look closely, you might be able to see its golden eyes. They come into my cottage during the autumn, and even more so in the garden shed, where they cluster together in large numbers hidden in old cardboard boxes and waiting for spring. They are one of the major friends of gardeners and do absolutely no harm indoors.

The alder fly is rather similar and abundant where there are alder trees. It might come in attracted by the light but doesn't really want to be there at all. Its body is dark and less delicate than the lacewing's; the wings have quite marked reddish-brown veins. Caddis flies are also sometimes

Adult lacewing

attracted to lighted windows; they are usually brownish, with long slender antennae and with four wings rather than two. They are utterly harmless in the house.

Mini flyers

Thunderflies or thunder bugs are alternative names for thrips, those tiny little black things that can devastate plants by sucking their juices (be they pea pods, grain or flowers) and often swarm on the sort of warm, still summer days that presage a noisy break in the weather. The females of some species come swarming indoors to hibernate and cover upstairs ceilings. If you examine them under a good magnifying glass or microscope (they are that tiny), you will see that they have long bodies, short antennae, a minute ovipostor for laying eggs in plants and two pairs of wings that are unlike what you'd expect a fly's wings to be: they are tiny and look more like feathers than wings (thrips are not flies). They won't do any harm indoors but it can be a bit tedious having to sweep up hundreds of minuscule corpses.

Moths

There are indoor moths that are simply irritants, with that infuriating habit of being attracted to artificial lighting at night and apparently trying to commit suicide against light bulbs and candle flames. The theories about why night-flying moths are so strongly attracted to light mainly revolve around using the moon as a navigational aid. It's usually male moths (the females have better things to do, like finding somewhere to lay their eggs outside). If you don't want to keep windows closed when you have the lights on in summer, it's perfectly simple to keep out moths with net curtains if they trouble you.

Anti-flies

There are plenty of anti-fly ideas. Older countrymen would always paint the inside of the cowshed blue, as flies seemed to dislike the 'colder' look of blue. Blue lightbulbs are said to have the same effect. Cottagers would hang bunches of mint or basil in the windows to deter flies, and also apparently bunches of nettles. If flies or mozzies bother you in the garden, rub your skin with fresh mint: it will smell much nicer than some of the insect repellents you can buy. Or you could take refuge under a walnut tree, which is somewhere flies never venture. Indoors, the main weapon against flies is tip-top hygiene.

Flies are very alert to a swipe but react less instantly to very slow movements. If you don't want to kill the poor little thing but just want to get it out of the house, obviously the first action is to open the window and shoo it out. If that is not an option, you can usually catch a fly by using a clear plastic pot of some kind, preferably square rather than round (so that it can get into corners), and move it very, very slowly towards the fly to cover it. Don't be tempted to slap the container down suddenly at the last moment because it is almost impossible to be quicker than a fly. Softee softee catchee fly: go so slowly that you are hardly moving the container at all, until the fly is safely underneath. Then slip a piece of stiff cardboard under the container and carry the fly away.

If you want to be really mean to a fly, squirt its wings with hairspray and it won't be able to fly.

Clothes moths are a different matter. The adults look so innocuous, not to say inconspicuous: they are small and buff-coloured and they much prefer to live indoors than out. Although they have perfectly normal wings, they are not very eager to fly: you are more likely to see them scuttling into a hiding place if disturbed. The main clothes moths have white larvae with brown heads. The larva makes itself a little shelter from the fibres of its favourite food (anything woollen or furry). You are most likely to see adult clothes moths in the summer but to find their eggs in warm, dark places in winter. You can destroy the eggs in carpets by covering the carpet with a damp cloth and pressing it with a hot iron until the cloth is dry.

Moths don't like the smell of cloves, lavender, orange peel, cedarwood or fresh bog myrtle and there are many other moth repellents on the market. Moths are less likely to attack stored clothes if the clothes are clean. Bear in mind that, before there were woollies and carpets, clothes moths usually laid their eggs in birds' nests.

Adult clothes moth and larva

BEETLES

This huge group includes things like weevils and cockroaches, and also lots of things that tunnel into your woodwork and furniture. It includes another regular house visitor: ladybirds, which might fancy hibernating in your loft or in crannies in the house. You often find that they return to the same site every year, sometimes in clusters. They do no harm at all indoors and a great deal of good in the garden, so let them be. Sometimes, if indoor ladybirds wake up too early to be let out, I offer them some home-made nectar (honey melted in water), which they seem to enjoy.

Less welcome, though for no good reason, were the black beetles that would always scurry about at night in downstairs rooms in an old and isolated cottage where I lived in the 'seventies. They would find their way in under draughty doors and often seemed suicidal, scuttling straight into the hot ashes of the inglenook fire. They were modest in size, certainly less than 2.5cm (1in) long, and harmless – probably a *Pterostichus* species of ground beetle doing me a favour by predating on various insects – but they certainly worried visitors.

Fabric beetles

If you think your woollens or carpets have been attacked by clothes moths, you might be wrong. The carpet beetle could be the culprit, or rather its 'woolly bear' larvae. Adult carpet beetles are harmless consumers of nectar and pollen but their larvae, in the wild, chew all sorts of things in birds' nests, especially feathers, but wool and fur will do nicely as substitutes (the same tastes as clothes moth larvae). The adults have a broad oval shape with a fuzzy and vaguely zigzag pattern. You will usually find them behind skirting-boards or

Carpet beetle larva, or 'woolly bear'

underneath fitted carpets, which means vacuuming both sides of the carpet and both sides of the underlay as well, and filling in any cracks in the floorboards below.

Museum collections can suffer badly from woolly bears, and also from clothes moths, silverfish and booklice. Sometimes they deal with a problem by deep-freezing whatever is infested, which kills off the culprit, or they use pheromone-baited sticky traps.

Kitchen beetles

The main indoor scuttler in kitchens is the cockroach, which can run at quite a pace. In Britain, which is not really warm enough for cockroaches, it is more likely to be a pest in restaurants and places where food is prepared for the public than in a domestic kitchen: it likes plenty of warmth, dark damp corners and a good supply of food. Its long antennae sweep backwards and it has long, spiky legs. Cockroaches are nocturnal animals, hiding during the day behind cupboards, under the refridgerator, or nice and snug by central-heating pipes. They are unhygienic and smelly; they are deemed to be vermin and should be trapped or destroyed. There are many ingenious traps for cockroaches; the simplest is a smooth-sided pie dish baited with jam or beer (they can't climb out of the dish again) and with an access ramp – but if you have an infestation, it should be dealt with by experts.

Larder or bacon beetles, flour beetles and mealworms (which are the larvae of the mealworm beetle and are sold in large numbers as fishing bait and, more recently, as live food for feeding garden birds) are more likely to be found in commercial premises than in kitchens. But you might find weevils, which are very small animals recognisable by their long snouts. They are essentially vegetarian and the numerous different species have different tastes. Some are grain specialists and might infest your flour or cereals. Other kitchen weevils like dried fruit or nuts. The legless larvae of some species chomp away inside growing vegetables, especially peas and broad beans (and nettles), and the adults of these sometimes find their way indoors in late summer. They might look rather like the dreaded wood-boring beetles but relax – they won't attack your furniture or house timbers.

Wood-boring beetles

This is where the real trouble begins. Wood-boring beetles, in nature, do a great job by breaking down deadwood. The trouble is that 'deadwood' is a correct description for house timbers: they are no longer part of a growing tree and are therefore a fair target for wood-borers. The major culprits in the home are furniture beetles, whose larvae tunnel into mainly coniferous timbers, and the dreaded death-watch beetle, whose larvae can reduce ancient oak beams to dust. Luckily, death-watch beetles are much rarer than furniture beetles.

Furniture beetles are about 2mm (1⁄16in) long and brown. Their larvae take up to three years to tunnel out. You will find a very small, clean hole – 1 to 2mm (1⁄32 to 1⁄16in) – and a little heap of what looks like fine sawdust (actually frass, or the grub's droppings), which is the first sign you will have of their presence, by which time the damage has been done and there are probably several more generations already at work deep within. The exit holes are made when the larvae emerge as adults, usually in June or July, and you might see them trying to crawl to freedom on the windowpanes. These will mainly be males, which will already have mated with emerging females, who will already be laying their eggs in the timbers.

When people talk about woodworm, they usually mean the larvae of the furniture beetle. Don't be fooled by the name 'furniture beetle': they are equally likely to attack house timbers, the unpainted under-edge of a door and untreated garden sheds. They won't attack painted wood. They are mainly a problem in softwood (i.e. conifer wood, such as pine) and will bore into anything that was felled more than about a decade ago. They prefer the timber to be a bit damp, which makes tunnelling easier. But if it's dry in a centrally heated home, it's just a bigger challenge in more comfortable surroundings.

Death-watch beetles at least have the courtesy to let you know they are in the house: they make tapping sounds in the spring to attract mates and when you hear the dreaded tap-tap-tap indoors, you know that these are beetles that have completed their larval stage, which means they have just tunnelled their way out of your beams or floorboards and the damage is done. You will soon find the very small, drab brown beetles crawling all over the place, especially at the windows and on the floor, trying to get out, or you might find what at first sight looks like old mouse droppings but on closer inspection are dead beetles that have failed to get out.

Once you have experienced death-watch beetles, you will lie awake at night listening for that Morse-like tapping, which seems much too loud to be made by such a small creature. Oak is their favourite, also other hardwoods – they

Death-watch beetle

are much less likely to attack the pine and deal that form the skeletons of so many more modern houses. The holes they leave when they emerge from the timber are 3 to 4mm (⅛ to ³⁄₁₆in) in diameter, which is about twice the size of those left by the furniture beetle.

Longhorn beetles have fat white grubs that attack both living and dead timber. They really prefer trees but if a tree has been felled for timber and happens to contain grubs, they will continue to chomp hidden within it for two or three years, by which time the timber might have been built into your house. The adult beetles are good flyers, with rather flattened bodies and the long antennae that give them the group its name. Some are black or dark in colour but others are quite exciting – like the black-and-yellow wasp beetle, the emerald or blue musk beetle, and others that are royal blue, scarlet or extravagantly patterned. You are far less likely to be accommodating longhorns or death-watch beetles than furniture beetles.

Because of the destruction that wood-borers can cause, you should have no hesitation in taking immediate measures to destroy them. While you might be able to deal with woodworm in furniture yourself, more radical treatment is needed if they are in structural timbers – in the roof, or the stairs, joists and floorboards, all of which are usually hidden from view. If the timber crumbles when you push a knife blade into it, you need expert help.

Longhorn beetle

You certainly need the experts when it comes to death-watch beetles: your entire house will have to be emptied and fumigated, and the smell of the fumigants will drive you as well as the beetles out of the house for some time. When death-watch beetles tap or you find evidence of longhorn beetles, contact the environmental health department of your local council immediately: they will be just as eager to get rid of them as you are, before they spread to other houses.

Remember that many commercial products will also be harmful to bats and you are legally obliged to take proper precautions, in terms of the product used and the timing of application, if bats live in your loft.

It is rather sad to end on this note of destruction, whereas the entire book has been devoted to dissuading rather than killing what you might consider to be pests. With virtually any other living creature that people automatically label as a 'pest', I would urge you to learn to live with them and come to find them interesting. Really, they have just as much right on this earth as we do and, very often, it is humans who are the true pests.

House spider

Useful Information

PUBLICATIONS

Ashby, Eric, *My Life with Foxes*, Robert Hale, London, 2000

Baxter, J, of Lewes, *Baxter's Library of Agricultural and Horticultural Knowledge* (3rd edn), Sussex Agricultural Press, 1834

Beebee, Trevor, *Frogs and Toads*, Whittet Books, London, 1985

Chinery, Michael, *Garden Creepy-Crawlies*, Whittet Books, London 1986

Coles, Charles, *Gardens and Deer: A Guide to Damage Limitation*, Swan Hill, Shrewsbury, 1997

Corbet, G B, & Southern, H N, *The Handbook of British Mammals* (3rd edn), Blackwell, Oxford, 1996

Flowerdew, John, *Mice and Voles*, Whittet Books, London, 1993

Harris, S, Jefferies, D, Cheeseman, C, & Booty, C, *Problems with Badgers?* (3rd edn), RSPCA, Horsham, West Sussex, 1994

Harris, Stephen, *Urban Foxes*, Whittet Books, London, 1986

Holm, Jessica, *Squirrels*, Whittet Books, London, 1987

Jacobs, Ruth, *Organic Gardening: A Guide for Beginners* (2nd edn), Alfresco Books, Warrington, Cheshire, 1999

Langton, Tom, *Snakes and Lizards*, Whittet Books, London, 1989

Lawrence, M J, & Brown, R W, *Mammals of Britain: Their Tracks, Trails and Signs*, Blandford Press, London, 1973

McBride, Ann, *Rabbits and Hares*, Whittet Books, London, 1988

MacDonald, D, & Doncaster, C P, *Foxes in your Neighbourhood?*, RSPCA, Horsham, West Sussex, 1985

Porter, Val, *RSPCA Guide to Garden Wildlife*, HarperCollins, London, 1996

Porter, Val, *Animal Rescue*, Ashford, Southampton, 1989

Prior, Richard, *Trees and Deer*, Swan Hill, Shrewsbury, 1994

Ratcliffe, P R, & Mayle, B A, *Roe Deer Biology and Management*, Forestry Commission: Bulletin 105, HMSO Publications, London, 1992

Richardson, Phil, *Bats*, Whittet Books, London, 1985

Stone, David R, *The Mole*, Shire Natural History, Princes Risborough, 1992

Thompson, Arthur R, *Nature by Night*, Ivor Nicholson & Watson, London, 1931

Tittensor, A M, & Lloyd, H G, *Rabbits*, Forestry Commission: Forestry Record 125, HMSO Publications, London, 1983

LEGAL INFORMATION

British Association for Shooting and Conservation, *Trapping Pest Birds: A Code of Practice*, Wrexham, 2001

Brooman, S, & Legge, D, *Law Relating to Animals*, Cavendish Publishing, London, 1997

Cooper, Margaret, *An Introduction to Animal Law*, Academic Press, London, 1987

Lorton, R, *A–Z Countryside Law*, Stationery Office, London, 2001

Palmer, J, *Animal Law: A Concise Guide to the Law Relating to Animals*, Shaw & Sons, Crayford, Kent, 2001

Parkes, C, & Thornley, J, *Fair Game*, Pelham, London, 1987

RSPB: *Wild Birds and the Law*, Sandy, Bedfordshire, 1998

ORGANIC AND BIOCONTROL CATALOGUES

The Organic Gardening Catalogue
Riverdene Business Park
Molesey Road
Hersham
Surrey
KT12 4RG

Tel: 01932 253666
Fax: 01932 252707
Email: chaseorg@aol.com
Web: www.OrganicCatalog.com

Pest Problem Solver Non-Chemical Solutions: Defenders Ltd
Occupation Road
Wye
Ashford
Kent
TN25 5EN

Tel: 01233 813121
Fax: 01233 813633
Web: www.defenders.co.uk

Green Gardener
41 Strumpshaw Road
Brundall
Norfolk
NR13 5PG

For natural pest control, tel: 01603 715096
For worm and wildlife products, tel: 01473 833031
Order and fax hotline, tel: 01603 716986
Web: www.greengardener.co.uk

ADDRESSES

National Federation of Badger Groups
15 Cloisters Business Centre
8 Battersea Park Road
London
SW8 4BG

Tel: 020 7498 3220
Fax: 020 7627 4212
Email: enquiries@nfbg.org.uk
Web: www.badger.org.uk

Bat Conservation Trust
15 Cloisters Business Centre
8 Battersea Park Road
London
SW8 4BG

Tel: 020 7627 2629
Fax: 020 7627 2628
Email: enquiries@bats.org.uk
Web: www.bats.org.uk

British Deer Society
Burgate Manor
Fordingbridge
Hampshire
SP6 1EF

Tel: 01425 655434
Fax: 01425 655433
Email: h.q@bds.org.uk
Web: www.bds.org.uk

British Hedgehog Preservation Society
Hedgehog House
Dhustone
Ludlow
Shropshire
SY8 3PL

Tel: 01584 890801
Email: bhps@dhustone.fsbusiness.co.uk
Web: www.software-technics.com/bhps

British Herpetological Society
c/o Zoological Society of London
Regent's Park
London
NW1 4RY

Tel: 020 8452 9578
Web: www.thebhs.org

British Trust for Ornithology
The Nunnery
Thetford
Norfolk
IP24 2PU

Tel: 01842 750050
Fax: 01842 750030
Email: info@bto.org
Web: www.bto.org

British Wildlife Rehabilitation Council
c/o RSPCA Wildlife Department
Wilberforce Way
Southwater
Horsham
West Sussex
RH13 9RH

Tel: 08705 555999
Web: www.bwrc.org.uk

Cats Protection
17 Kings Road
Horsham
West Sussex
RH13 5PN

Tel: 01403 221900
Fax: 01403 218414
National Helpline: 01403 221919
Email: cpl@cats.org.uk
Web: www.cats.org.uk

English Nature
Northminster House
Peterborough
PE1 1UA

Tel: 01733 455101
Fax: 01733 455103
Email: enquiries@english-nature.org.uk
Web: www.english-nature.org.uk

Froglife
Mansion House
27–28 Market Place
Halesworth
Suffolk
IP19 8AY

Tel: 01986 873733
Fax: 01986 874744
Email: froglife@froglife.org.uk
Web: www.froglife.org.uk

Mammal Society
15 Cloisters House
8 Battersea Park Road
London
SW8 4BG

Tel: 020 7498 4358
Fax: 020 7622 8722
Email: enquiries@mammal.org.uk
Web: www.mammal.org.uk

Otter Trust
Earsham
Bungay
Norfolk
NR35 2AF

Tel: 01986 893470
Fax: 01986 892461
Web: www.ottertrust.org.uk

**Royal Society for the Prevention of Cruelty to Animals
(RSPCA)**
Wilberforce Way
Southwater
Horsham
West Sussex
RH13 7WN

Tel: 0870 010 1181
Fax: 0870 753 0048
Email: enquiries@rspca.org.uk
Web: www.rspca.org.uk

Royal Society for the Protection of Birds (RSPB)
The Lodge
Sandy
Bedfordshire
SG19 2DL

Tel: 01767 680551
Fax: 01767 692365
Email: enquiries@rspb.org.uk
Web: www.rspb.org.uk

Index